A Concise Dictionary of
ABBREVIATIONS

A Concise Dictionary of

ABBREVIATIONS

Compiled and edited by

GEORGE MAYBERRY

TUDOR PUBLISHING COMPANY
New York

Designed by Bernard Lipsky

Library of Congress Catalog Card Number: 61-9227
Printed in the United States of America
by Ganis & Harris, New York

Acknowledgments

The staffs of the New York Public Library,
the Library of Congress,
the Government Printing Office,
the New York Times,
the Tudor Publishing Company,
particularly John J. Ermatinger,
Josephine Frank of the United Nations,
US ARMY INFORMATION OFFICE
and
R. L. BUFKINS
CDR   USN
Head
Magazine & Book Branch

Introduction

THE ORIGIN OF ABBREVIATIONS, as with the origin of most cultural phenomena, is lost in time. In the earliest recorded instances, it would appear that then as now the primary purpose of the abbreviation was to save time, space and, one would presume, energy, in the case of the artisan who carved uncial or lapidary letters on monuments or coins. Another purpose which persists today was euphemism. The Hebrew tetragrammaton **IHVH**, or **JHVH**, etc. was employed for the name of the supreme being which was too sacred to pronounce; a less sublime euphemistic usage is the more recent **g.d.**

SPQR and **I.N.R.I.** are full-blown examples of the most common form of the abbreviation, the initial letter standing for the word. Initials, abridgments and contractions are all present in the work of the first great "inventors" of abbreviations, the copiers and monastic scribes of the Middle Ages. Indeed, the modern science of paleography would be unthinkable without a thorough knowledge of ancient abbreviations. The introduction of printing reduced the use of abbreviations in some fields, but by and large they have not only persisted but proliferated. An effort by the British parliament in the eighteenth century to forbid their use in legal documents attests to their vitality, and in our time we have seen at least one new form of abbreviation take root and flower: the acronym, where initials or initial syllables of the words of a compound term combine to form a new name (**Waves, Cominform**). It should be noted that certain of these abbreviations have passed into common usage as words in their own right, and are no longer the special province of what Eric Partridge calls "abbreviology."

This dictionary aims to be precisely what it calls itself. "Concise" in the sense that it is as short as a book that attempts to list all important abbreviations in general use can be. By "abbreviation" we mean the common shortened form of a word or phrase. Now a certain arbitrariness had to be observed in both instances. Thus "general use" excludes the usages of special fields that are rarely if ever of use to someone outside that field. We do not attempt, for example, to include all the abbreviations contained in the *Concise Chemical and Technical Dictionary* (a volume which runs to over a thousand pages in spite of the title), but we list the symbols of all chemical elements and abbreviations for other chemical terms and usages of possible interest to more than the specialist. Large organizations such as the United States Army have developed an immense vocabulary of abbreviations, but it is doubtful that the general reader will encounter **EZAACMO** or **RQSTFOLINFO**. **WAF** and **WO** we may meet, however, and it is fitting to have them in GI style.

At this point it is well to insist that the function of this book, like that of any other dictionary, is as a guide book, not a rule book. We have, however, attempted to give preferred forms for the abbreviations listed here. Whenever possible, as with **GI** or **UN**, we will give the form used by the organization that employs it. Otherwise (and the two are not mutually exclusive) historical principles or the usages of received authority prevail. We have indicated our impatience with many abbreviations, but have resisted the impulse to eliminate them wherever the rubric of common usage indicates we are still overruled. These various considerations should explain why more than one form is listed in some cases.

We have seen in our time, beginning with the alphabetizing

activities of the New Deal and continental European practice followed by the UN, a so-called "modern" practice of eliminating the period entirely and using capitals almost exclusively in all abbreviations. But for the British and for us, the House of Commons is still the **H.C.** even though its members still refer — incorrectly by the principle listed above — to the **U.N.** and sometimes even to **U.N.R.R.A.** And they are upheld by the **A.I.C.E.** in referring to a **B.t.u.** which they would never confuse with a **B.T.U.**

This is not cantankerous hair-splitting. On the contrary, abbreviations have a precise orthography, allowing as with full words, variants for reasons of history and usage. Let us, for example, see what the "modern" practice does to the usability of the first and third letters of the alphabet when it omits the period. It is reduced to

>**ac** acre; alternating current
>
>**Ac** actinium
>
>**AC** alternating current (preferred); Aviation Cadet (US Army); etc.
>
>**aC** (this stands for nothing)

only two of which are recognizable abbreviations.

By the "old" method (which always has room for the "new" when it is appropriate) we have these possibilities

>**ac** alternating current
>
>**ac.** acre
>
>**a.c.** alternating current
>
>**Ac** actinium
>
>**AC** alternating current (preferred); Aviation Cadet; etc.
>
>**A.C.** Athletic Club, as in N.Y.A.C.

and we would still have **a.C.** and **aC.** if we had a use for them.

We hope furthermore that the reader will agree that more than utility and clarification will be sacrificed if the growing trend reduces **Sa, SA, S.A., s.a.** to just the conformist **SA.**

In "streamlining" abbreviations, the "modern" practice has — again a rather mixed blessing — speeded up the formation of acronyms. Some like **asdic** and **sonar** have become word entities; others like **ASCAP** and **UNESCO** may still be thought of primarily as abbreviations although they are pronounced as words also. Others like **SPARS** ("Semper Paratus — Always Ready") for the Women's Coast Guard Reserve could only have been invented, as was in reverse the title for the organization Women Accepted for Volunteer Emergency Service to make the abbreviation **WAVES**. For our purposes, acronyms are listed only when they are still clearly abbreviations.

Other shortened forms, particularly in the realm of slang, are not necessarily abbreviations in any strict sense: e.g. *bennies* for benzedrine or *Monkey Ward* for Montgomery Ward & Co. Where the familiar shortened form is identical with the abbreviation it will usually be retained here: e.g. **A & P**, the **Y**. One example will suffice to show how far afield a concise dictionary would have had to go if we were to attempt to satisfy all claims between short forms. In New Jersey, "the DL&W" is employed interchangeably with "the Lackawanna" (never "the Delaware" or "the Delly" for the Delaware, Lackawanna and Western Railroad Company). However, "the New Haven" is the universal short form for the New York, New Haven and Hartford Railroad Company.

A dictionary is a living thing. Following the example of the Oxford *Authors' & Printers' Dictionary*, to which we are indebted in many other ways, we have included blank pages for notes and addenda.

George Mayberry

New York,
New York

A Note on the Use of this Book

The General Index which starts on page 67 gives in most instances simply a concise definition of the abbreviation. If the term you are looking up falls in one of the special lists (see Contents) there may be more information on it at that place.

The Bibliography on page 159 will be of value for abbreviations in general; those appended to the notes preceding the special lists are exhaustive for the specific field, with the exception noted for Scientific and Technical Terms.

Contents

Introduction .... page 7

Selected Listings (with selected bibliographies)

    Degrees, Decorations and Designations 15

    Geography, Peoples and Languages 25

    Military Terms 35

    Religious Terms 43

    Scientific and Technical Terms 51

General Index 67

General Bibliography 159

Degrees, Decorations and Designations

These are the initials you will frequently encounter after the name of an author or the speaker of the evening, and increasingly wherever a professional person is listed in print. This procedure is still less usual in the democratic United States than in Europe (and particularly in the British Isles). We have, however, attempted to compensate for our abolition of feudal rankings with symbols of our trades and callings.

N.B. Members of some groups (**A.I.D.** for example) simply list the initials of the organization after their names; others precede the initials of the organization or group with **F**(ellow) or **M**(ember). If you do not find the initials you are trying to identify here, try the military and religious listings.

Bibliography:
The International Who's Who.
Who's Who.
Who's Who in America.

Degrees, Decorations and Designations

A.A. Associate in Arts

A.B. *Artium Baccalaureus* (L.) Bachelor of Arts; see **B.A.**

A.E. and P. Ambassador Extraordinary and Plenipotentiary

A.M. *Artium Magister* (L.) Master of Arts; see **M.A.**

A.M.I.C.E. Associate Member of the Institution of Civil Engineers

A.M.I.E.E. Associate Member of the Institution of Electrical Engineers

A.M.I.Mech.E. Associate Member of the Institution of Mechanical Engineers

A.R.A. Associate of the Royal Academy

B.A. *Baccalaureus Artium* (L.) Bachelor of Arts (This is the equivalent of **A.B.** The order of the initials depends upon the whim or practice of the institution of higher learning granting it.)

B. Agr. *Baccalaureus Agriculturae* (L.) Bachelor of Agriculture

B. Ag. Sc. Bachelor of Agricultural Science

B.Arch. Bachelor of Architecture

Bart. Baronet

B.B.A. Bachelor of Business Administration

B.C. Bachelor of Chemistry

B.C.E. Bachelor of Chemical Engineering; Bachelor of Civil Engineering

B. Ch. *Baccalaureus Chirurgiae* (L.) Bachelor of Surgery. Don't be frightened by this one, or **B.D.S.** below. These are highly qualified British technicians.

B.C.L. Bachelor of Civil Law

B.D. *Baccalaureus Divinitatis* (L.) Bachelor of Divinity

B.D.S. Bachelor of Dental Surgery

B.E. Bachelor of Education; Bachelor of Engineering

B.F.A. Bachelor of Fine Arts gineering

B.E.M. British Empire Medal

B. ès L. *Bachelier ès Lettres* (F.) Bachelor of Letters

B. ès S. *Bachelier ès Sciences* (F.) Bachelor of Science

B.F. Bachelor of Finance; Bachelor of Forestry

B.F.A. Bachelor of Fine Arts

B.J. Bachelor of Journalism

B.L. Bachelor of Laws; Bachelor of Literature

B. Lit(t)., B. Lit. *Baccalaureus Lit(t)eratum* (L.) Bachelor of Literature

B.L.S. Bachelor of Library Science

B.M. *Baccalaureus Medicinae* (L.) Bachelor of Medicine; *Baccalaureus Musicae* (L.) Bachelor of Music

B.M.E. Bachelor of Mining Engineering

B. Mech. E. Bachelor of Mechanical Engineering

B. Mus. Bachelor of Music

B.P. *Baccalaureus Pharmiciae* (L.) Bachelor of Pharmacy

B. Pd., B. Pe. Bachelor of Pedagogy

B.S. Bachelor of Science; Bachelor of Surgery

B.Sc. *Baccalaureus Scientiae* (L.) Bachelor of Science

B.S.Ed. Bachelor of Science in Education

B.T., B.Th. *Baccalaureus Theologiae* (L.) Bachelor of Theology

Bt. Baronet

C.A. Chartered Accountant

C.B. *Chirurgiae Baccalaureus* (L.) Bachelor of Surgery; Companion of the Bath

C.B.E. Commander of the British Empire

C.E. Chemical Engineer; Civil Engineer

C.G. Consul General

Ch. D. Doctor of Chemistry

Ch. E., Chem. E. Chemical Engineer

C.J. Chief Justice

C.L.D. Doctor of Civil Law

C.L.U. Chartered Life Underwriter

C.M. *Chirurgiae Magister* (L.) Master in Surgery

C.M.G. Companion of the Order of St. Michael and St. George

CNO Chief of Naval Operations

CO Commanding Officer

C.P.A. Certified Public Accountant

C.S.A. Confederate States of America

C.S.D. Doctor of Christian Science

C.V.O. Commander of the (Royal) Victorian Order

D.A. District Attorney

D.Agr. Doctor of Agriculture

D.A.R. Daughters of the American Revolution

D.Arch. Doctor of Architecture

D.B.E. Dame (Commander of the) British Empire

D.C. Doctor of Chiropractic

D.C.L. Doctor of Civil Law

D.C.M. Distinguished Conduct Medal (U.S.)

D.D. *Divinitatis Doctor* (L.) Doctor of Divinity

D.D.S. Doctor of Dental Surgery. This degree is designated **D.M.D.** at Harvard and Tufts

D.D.Sc. Doctor of Dental Science

D.E. Doctor of Engineering; Doctor of Entomology

D.Eng. Doctor of Engineering

D.H.L. Doctor of Hebrew Literature

D.J. disc jockey (also **deejay**); District Judge; *Doctor Juris* (L.) Doctor of Law; see also **J.D.**

D.J.S. Doctor of Juridical Science

D.Lit., D.Litt *Doctor Lit(t)erarum* (L.) Doctor of Literature or Letters

D.L.S. Doctor of Library Science

D.M. Doctor of Mathematics; Doctor of Medicine; Doctor of Music

D.M.S. Director of Medical Services; Doctor of Medical Sciences

D.Mus. Doctor of Music

D.O. Doctor of Optometry; Doctor of Osteopathy

D.P.H. Diploma in Public Health; Doctor of Public Health

D.Phil. Doctor of Philosophy

D.S. Doctor of Science

D.S.C. Distinguished Service Cross

D.S.M. Distinguished Service Medal

D.S.O. Distinguished Service Order

D.S.T. Doctor of Sacred Theology

D.V.M. Doctor of Veterinary Medicine

Ed.B. Bachelor of Education

Ed.D. Doctor of Education

Ed.M. Master of Education

Esq. Esquire. A purely honorific title, usually used only in correspondence

F. Fellow (see note at head of this section)

F.A.A.A.S. Fellow of the American Association for the Advancement of Science; Fellow of the American Academy of Arts and Sciences

F.B.A. Fellow of the British Academy

F.F.V. First Families of Virginia; the social elect, often used sarcastically

F.H.S. Fellow of the Heraldry Society; Fellow of the Horticultural Society

F.R.A. Fellow of the Royal Academy (thus **F.R.C.S.** is Fellow of the Royal College of Surgeons, etc.)

F.S.Arch. Fellow of the Society of Architects

F.S.C. Brothers of the Christian Schools (Christian Brothers)

G.A.R. Grand Army of the Republic. (United States Civil War)

G.B.E. Knight (or Dame) Grand Cross of the British Empire

G.C.B. Grand Cross of the Bath

G.M.B. Grand Master of the Bath

H.B.M. His (or Her) Britannic Majesty

H.C.M. His (or Her) Catholic Majesty

J.D. *Juris Doctor* (L.) Doctor of Law

J.P. Justice of the Peace

J.S.D. Doctor of Juridical Science

K.B. Knight of the Bath

K.C. King's Counsel

K.G. Knight of the Garter

L.H.D. *Litterarum Humaniorum Doctor* (L.) Doctor of Humanities

Litt. D. *Litterarum Doctor* (L.) Doctor of Letters

LL.D. *Legum Doctor* (L.) Doctor of Laws

M. Master; Member. See note at heading of this section

M.A. *Magister Artium* (L.) Master of Arts

M.D. *Medicinae Doctor* (L.) Doctor of Medicine

M.F.A. Master of Fine Arts

M.F.H. Master of Fox Hounds

M.H. Medal of Honor (U.S.)

M.I.C.E. Member of the Institute of Civil Engineers (N.B. See also **M.I. Chem. E.,** etc. See above under **F**(ellow)

M.P. Member of Parliament; Military Police

M.R.A.S. Member of the Royal Academy of Sciences

M.S. Master of Science

N.A. National Academician

N.P. Notary Public

O.B.E. Officer of the British Empire

O.F.M. Order of Friars Minor (Franciscan) see under **Religious terms** for other **O**(rders)

Phar.B., Phar.D. Phar.M. Bachelor, Doctor, Master of Pharmacy

Ph.D. *Philosophiae Doctor* (L.) Doctor of Philosophy

P.L. Poet Laureate

P.M. Postmaster; Prime Minister; Provost Marshal

P.M.G. Post Master General

Q.C. Queen's Counsel

R.A. Royal Academician (for **R**(oyal) see **F.** and **M.**)

R.N. Registered Nurse

S.A.R. Sons of the American Revolution

S.B. Bachelor of Science

Sc.D. *Scientiae Doctor* (L.) Doctor of Science

S.J. Society of Jesus, Jesuit Fathers

S.P.A.S. *Societatis Philosophicae Americanae Socius* (L.) Member of the American Philosophical Society

S.S.D. *Sacrae Scripturae Doctor* (L.) Doctor of Sacred Scripture

S.T.D. *Scientiae Theologicae Doctor* (L.) Doctor of Theology

Th.D. Doctor of Theology

V.P. Vice President. Expanded affectionately to "Veep" for Mr. V.P. Barkley (1949)

VIP very important person. Although GPO does not give periods for this abbreviation, it is almost always "spelled" out V.I.P.; rarely pronounced or written **vip,** except as the signature of the cartoonist **v**(irgil) **i p**(artch)

Geography, Peoples and Languages

Nowhere in the realm of abbreviations is the exhortation "When in doubt, spell it out" more pertinent than when we come to geography, as any postal authority will be happy to inform you. So, if you don't find abbreviations in the following list for Bali, Chad, Iowa, Mali, or Sligo, there happily are none that have achieved even such frowned-upon usages (but here noted because some people insist upon using them) as *O.* for Ohio, *Cal.* instead of **Calif.**, and the ridiculous *Chl.* for Chile. Since, as we have noted before, dictionaries to be useful must be guidebooks, not rule books, and since people have insisted on using misleading and illogical procedures, we can only deplore but go on recording. And can only add "Alas!" for Alaska.

Bibliography:
Webster's *Geographical Dictionary* and Lippincott's *New Gazetteer.*
Worldmark Encyclopedia of the Nations (Harper)

Geography, Peoples and Languages

Aber. Aberdeen (Scotland)

AF. Anglo-French

Af. Africa; African; Afrikaans (South African Dutch)

Afg. Afghanistan

Afr. Africa; African

Agua. Aguascalientes (Mexico)

AL. Anglo-Latin

Ala. Alabama

Alas. Alaska

Alb. Albania; Albanian; Albany; Alberta

Alba. Alberta

Alg. Algeria

Alta. Alberta

Amer. America; American

Am. Ind. American Indian (language)

Amst. Amsterdam

A.N. Anglo-Norman

And. Andorra

Ang. Anglesey (Wales)

Ant. Antarctica; Antrim (Ireland)

Ar. Arabian; Arabic; Aramaic

Arab. Arabian; Arabic

Aram. Aramaic

Arg. Argentina; Argentine; Argyll (Scotland)

Ariz. Arizona

Ark. Arkansas

Arm. Armagh (Ireland)

Armen. Armenian

AS. Anglo-Saxon

As. Asia; Asian; Asiatic

Assyr. Assyrian

Atl. Atlantic

Aus. Australia

Aust. Austria; Austrian

Austl., Austral. Australia; Australasia

Az. Is. Azores Islands

Azo. Azores

B. British

B.A. Buenos Aires

Bab. Babylonian

Ba. Is. Bahama Islands

Bal. Baluchistan (part of Pakistan)

Barb. Barbados

Bas. Basutoland

Bav. Bavaria

B.C. British Columbia

Bech. Bechuanaland

Beds Bedfordshire (England)

Belg. Belgian; Belgium

Belg. Cong. Belgian Congo. (Now Independent Congo Republic)

BENELUX Belgium-The Netherlands-Luxemburg

Beng. Bengali

Ber. Berlin; Bermuda

Ber. Is. Bermuda Islands

Berks Berkshire (England)

Berw. Berwick (Scotland)

Bhu. Bhutan

Bol. Bolivia

Br. British

Braz. Brazil; Brazilian

Brec. Brecknockshire (Wales)

Br. Gu. British Guiana

Br. Hond. British Honduras

Br. Som. British Somaliland

Brit. Britain; British

Bucks Buckinghamshire (England)

Bulg. Bulgaria; Bulgarian

Bur. Burma

B.W.I. British West Indies

Byz. Byzantine; Byzantium

C. Celtic

C.A. Central America

Caern. Caernarvonshire (Wales)

Caith. Caithness (Scotland)

Cal. California

Calif. California (preferred)

Cam. Cameroons

Camb. Cambridge

Cambs. Cambridgeshire (England)

Camp. Campeche (Mexico)

Can. Canada; Canadian

Can. F. Canadian French

Can. Is. Canary Islands

Cant. Canterbury; Cantonese

Car. Carlow (Ireland)

Card. Cardiganshire (Wales)

C. B. I. Cape Breton Islands

Cel. Celebes

Celt. Celtic

Cen. Amer. Central America

Cey(l). Ceylon

Ch. China; Chinese

Chald. Chaldaic; Chaldee

Ches(h). Cheshire (England)

Chi. Chicago

Chia. Chiapas (Mexico)

Chih. Chihuahua (Mexico)

Chin. China; Chinese

Chin-Jap. Chino-Japanese

Chl. Chile

C.I. Channel Islands

Cla. Clackmannon (Scotland)

Coa. Coahila (Mexico)

Col. Colombia; Colorado

Colim. Colima (Mexico)

Colo. Colorado

Conn. Connecticut

Cont. Continental (Europe)

Cop., Copt. Coptic

Cor. Corsica

Corn., Cornw. Cornwall (England)

C.R. Costa Rica

Ct. Connecticut

Cumb Cumberland (England)

Cur. Curacao

C.V.Is. Cape Verde Islands

Cyp. Cyprian; Cypriote; Cyprus

C.Z. Canal Zone

Czech. Czechoslovakia

Dan. Danish

D.C. District of Columbia

D.E.I. Dutch East Indies

Del. Delaware

Denb., Denbh. Denbigshire (Wales)

Derby Derbyshire (England)

Derry Londonderry (Ireland)

Dev., Devon. Devonshire (England)

D.F. *District Federale,* (Federal District, Mexico)

Dom. Rep. Dominican Republic

Don. Donegal (Ireland)

Dorset Dorsetshire (England)

Dub. Dublin (Ireland, city & county)

Dumb. Dumbarton (Scotland)

Dumf. Dumfries (Scotland)

Dur. Durango (Mexico); Durham (England)

E. English

Ecua. Ecuador

Eg. Egypt; Egyptian

E. I. East Indian; East Indies

E.L. East Lothian (Scotland)

Eng. England; English

Ess. Essex (England)

Est. Estonia

Eth. Ethiopia

Eur. Europe; European

F. France; French

Falk. Is. Falkland Islands

Fin. Finland; Finnish

Fl. Flanders; Flemish

Fla. Florida

Flint. Flintshire (Wales)

Fr. France; French

Fr. Gu. French Guiana

Fr. Som. French Somaliland

Fris., Frs. Frisian

G. German

Ga. Gallic; Georgia

Gal. Galway (Ireland)

Gael. Gaelic

G.B. Great Britain

Gen. Geneva

Ger. Germany

Gib. Gibraltar

Gk. Greek

Glam., Glamorg. Glamorganshire (Wales)

Glos. Gloucestershire (England)
Gr. Grecian; Greece; Greek
Gr. Br. Great Britain
Grc. Greece
Grnld. Greenland
Guan. Guanajuato (Mexico)
Guat. Guatemala
Guer. Guerrero

Hai. Haiti
Hants Hampshire (England)
Heref. Herefordshire (England)
Herts Hertfordshire (England)
Hid. Hidalgo (Mexico)
Hond. Honduras
Hong K. Hong Kong
Hung. Hungarian; Hungary

Ice. Iceland; Icelandic
IDP International Driving Permit
IE, I.E. Indo-European
I.F.S. Irish Free State
I.G. Indo-Germanic
Ill. Illinois
I.M. Isle of Man
Ind. India; Indian; Indiana; Indies
Inv. Inverness
I.O.W. Isle of Wight
Ir. Ireland; Irish
Iran. Iranian
Ire. Ireland
Isr. Israel

It., Ital. Italian; Italy
I.W. Isle of Wight (England)
Jal. Jalisco (Mexico)
Jam. Jamaica
Jap. Japan; Japanese
Jav. Javanese

Kans., Kan., Kas. Kansas
Kild. Kildare (Ireland)
Kilk. Kilkenny (Ireland)
Kin. Kinross (Scotland)
Kinc. Kincardinel (Scotland)
Kirk. Kirkcudbright (Scotland)
Kuw. Kuwait
Ky. Kentucky

L. Latin
La. Louisiana
Lab. Labrador
Lancs Lancashire (England)
Lat. Latin
Latv. Latvia
LD., LD, L.D. Low Dutch
Leics. Leicestershire (England)
Leit. Leitrim (Ireland)
LG, LG., L.G. Low German
L.I. Long Island
Lib. Liberia
Lim. Limerick (Ireland)
Lincs Lincolnshire (England)
Lith. Lithuania; Lithuanian
Lnrk. Lanark (Scotland)

Long. Longford (Ireland)

Lou. Louth (Ireland)

Lux. Luxemburg

M. Manitoba (Canada)

Madag. Madagascar

Mal. Malta

Man. Manitoba

Mass. Massachusetts

Md. Maryland

ME, ME., M.E. Middle English

Me. Maine

Mea. Meath (Ireland)

Medit. Mediterranean

Meri. Merionethshire (Wales)

Mex. Mexican; Mexico (also a state); but please don't refer to a Mexican national in this fashion

MHG. MHG., M.H.G. Middle High German

Mich. Michigan; Michoacan (Mexico)

Middlx., Midx., Mx. Middlesex (England)

Mid.L. Midlothian (Scotland)

Miss. Mississippi

Minn. Minnesota

Mo. Missouri

Mon. Monaghan (Ireland)

Mong. Mongolia

Mon., Mons. Monmouthshire (England)

Mont. Montana

Mont., Montgom. Montgomeryshire (Scotland)

Mor. Morocco

Morel. Morelos (Mexico)

Moz. Mozambique

N. Norse

N.B. New Brunswick

N.C. North Carolina

N. Dak. North Dakota

N.E. New England

Nebr. Nebraska

Nep. Nepal

Neth. Netherlands

Neth. Gu. Netherlands Guiana

Neth. Ind. Netherlands Indies

Nev. Nevada

Newf. Newfoundland

New M. New Mexico

N.F. Newfoundland; Norman French

NGr, NGr., N.Gr. New Greek

N.H. New Hampshire

NHG, NHG., N.H.G. New High German

Nicar. Nicaragua

Nig. Nigeria

N. Ire. Northern Ireland

N.J. New Jersey

NL, NL., N.L. New Latin

N.M. New Mexico

N. Mex. New Mexico

Nor. Norman; North; Norway; Norwegian

Norf. Norfolk

Northants Northamptonshire

Northum(b). Northumberland

Notts Nottinghamshire

N. Rh. Northern Rhodesia

Norw. Norway

N.S. Nova Scotia

N.S.W. New South Wales

N.W.T. Northwest Territory (Canada)

N.Y. New York

Nyas. Nyasaland

N.Z., N. Zeal. New Zealand

O. Ocean; Ohio (not official); Ontario

Oax. Oaxaca (Mexico)

OE, OE., O.E. Old English

OF, OF., O.F. Old French

Off. Offaly (Ireland)

OHG, OHG., O.H.G. Old High German

Okla. Oklahoma

ON, O.N. Old Norse

Ont. Ontario (Canada)

Ore. Oregon

Oreg. Oregon (preferred)

Ork. Orkney (Scotland)

OS, OS., O.S. Old Saxon

Oxf., Ox. Oxford

Oxf., Oxon Oxfordshire (England)

Oxon. Oxonia (L.) Oxford; Bishop of Oxford

Pa. Pennsylvania

Pac., Pacif. Pacific

Pal. Palestine

Pan. Panama

Para. Paraguay

Peeb. Peebles (Scotland)

P.E.I. Prince Edward Island (Canada)

Pemb. Pembrokeshire (Wales)

Pen., pen. peninsula

Penn., Penna. Pennsylvania

Pers. Persia; Persian

Peruv. Peruvian

Pg. Portugal; Portuguese

Phil. Philippine

Phila. Philadelphia

Phil. I., Phil. Is. Philippine Islands

P.I. Philippine Islands

Pol. Poland; Polish

Port. Portugal; Portuguese

P.Q. Province of Quebec (Canada)

Pr. Provencal

P.R. Puerto Rico

Prov. Provencal

Prus., Pruss. Prussia; Prussian

Pueb. Puebla (Mexico)

Q. Quebec

Que. Quebec

Quer. Queretaro (Mexico)

Rad. Radnorshire (Wales)

Rens. Rensfrew (Scotland)

R.I. Rhode Island

ROK Republic of Korea

Ros. Roscommon (Ireland)

Ross. Ross & Cromarty (Scotland)

Roum. Roumania; Roumanian

Rox. Roxburgh

Rum. Rumania; Rumanian

Rus., Russ. Russia; Russian

Rut., Rutd., Rutl. Rutlandshire (England)

S.A. South Africa; South America: South Australia

S.Afr., S. Afr. South Africa

Salop Shropshire (England)

S. Am., S. Amer. South America; South American

Sam. Samaritan; Samoa

Sans., Sansk. Sanskrit

Sard. Sardinia

Sask. Saskatchewan

Sau.Ar. Saudi Arabia

Sax. Saxon; Saxony

Sc. Scotch; Scots; Scottish

S.C. South Carolina

Scan., Scand. Scandinavia

Scot. Scotch; Scotland; Scottish

S. Dak. South Dakota

Selk. Selkirk (Scotland)

Sem. Semitic

Serb. Serbia; Serbian

Shet. Shetland (Scotland)

S.I. Sandwich Islands; Staten Island (N.Y.)

Sic. Sicilian; Sicily

Sin. Sinaloa (Mexico)

Skr. Sanskrit

Skt. Sanskrit

Slav. Slavic; Slavonian

S.L.P. San Lusi Potosi (Mexico)

S.Mar. San Marino

Som., Somerset Somersetshire (England)

Son. Sonora (Mexico)

Sp. Spain; Spaniard; Spanish

S.Rh. Southern Rhodesia

Staffs Staffordshire (England)

Stir. Stirling (Scotland)

Suff. Suffolk (England)

Sur. Surrey (England)

Sus. Sussex (England)

Suth. Sutherland (Scotland)

Sw., Swed. Sweden; Swedish

Switz, Swit., Swtz. Switzerland

Syr. Syria

Tam. Tamaulipas (Mexico)

Tan. Tanganyika

Tas(m). Tasmania

Tenn. Tennessee

Teut. Teuton; Teutonic

Tex. Texan; Texas

T.H. Territory of Hawaii

Thai. Thailand (formerly Siam)

Tib. Tibet

Tip. Tipperary (Ireland)

T.T. Tanganyika Territory

Tun. Tunisia

Turk. Turkey; Turkish

Tyr. Tyrone (Ireland)

UAR United Arab Republic

Ug. Uganda

U.K. United Kingdom (of Great Britain and Northern Ireland)

Ukr. Ukraine

U.S.Afr., U. of S. Afr. Union of South Africa

Uru. Uruguay

U.S., US United States

U.S.A. Union of South Africa; United States of America

Ut. Utah (not official)

Va. Virginia

Ven. Venice

Venez. Venezuela

Ver. Vera Cruz (Mexico)

V.I. Virgin Islands

Vict. Victoria (Australia)

Vt. Vermont

W. Wales; Washington; Welsh

W.A. West Africa; Western Australia

Wal. Walloon

Wal., Walach. Walachian

War Warwickshire (England)

Wash. Washington

Wat. Waterford (England)

Westm. Westminster; Westmorland (England) Westmeath (Ireland)

Wex. Wexford (Ireland)

W.I. West Indies

Wick. Wicklow (Ireland)

Wig. Wigtown (Scotland)

Wilts. Wiltshire (England)

Wis., Wisc. Wisconsin

W.L. West Lothian (Scotland)

Worcs Worcestershire (England)

W. Va. West Virginia

Wyo., Wy. Wyoming

Yem. Yemen

Yidd. Yiddish

Yks. Yorkshire

Yorks Yorkshire (England)

Y.T. Yukon Territory (Canada)

Yuc. Yucatan

Yugo. Yugoslavia

Yuk. Yukon

Zac. Zacatecas (Mexico)

Zan. Zanzibar

Military Terms

Military terms are a great source of abbreviations, particularly acronyms, because (1) combat communications require brevity and accuracy; (2) cataloguing nomenclature is an exacting and exhausting job, even with abbreviations; and (3) many scientific advancements are developed for the military (**radar, sonar, jato,** etc.) and passed on to private industry. We include such acronyms, noting the torturous route that some, like **WAVES** and **SPARS,** had to follow. Included, too, are some British military terms. whose abbreviations differ from ours primarily by having periods (or "points" to lexicographers). Thus, General Headquarters is **GHQ** (US Army) and **G.H.Q.** (Brit.). And because interest in our Civil War is at its zenith, we include historical military terms such as **brevet** and **brevetted,** which are no longer current. (An addition which is not listed in Army Regulations but which may be familiar to the reader is **KP,** the unsung but unforgettable duty of the citizen-soldier.) N.B. The military, the USN in particular, does not always substitute the exact initials for the words abbreviated. See **AG** for Aerographer's Mate, **AK** for Aviation Storekeeper, etc.

Bibliography:
Military Terms, Abbreviations, and Symbols (AR 320-50)
The Blue Jackets Manual
The Navy Blue Book

Military Terms

A Army

AA Airman Apprentice (USN); antiaircraft

AAA antiaircraft artillery (US Army)

AACS U.S. Airforce Airways and Air Communications Service, formerly, Army Air

AAF Army Airfield

AB Aviation Boatswain's Mate (USN)

abn airborne

AC Air Controlman (USN)

ADC Air Defense Command

Adj. Gen. Adjutant General

AE Aviation Electrician's Mate (USN)

A.E.F. American Expeditionary Forces

AF Air Force (USAF); Aviation Photographer's Mate (USN)

A.F. Army form

AFB Air Force base

AFUS Air Force of the United States (US Army)

AG Aerographer's Mate (USN); Adjutant General

AGCT Army General Classifications Test

AGS Army General Staff

AHQ Army Headquarters

AK Aviation Storekeeper (USN)

AL Aviation Electronicsman (USN)

AM Aviation Structural Mechanic (USN)

ammo ammunition (US Army)

AMEDS Army Medical Service

AMTRAC amphibious tractor (US Army)

AN Airman (USN)

ANC Army Nurse Corps

ANG Air National Guard

ANZAC Australian and New Zealand Army Corps (an early acronym)

AO Aviation Ordnanceman (USN); Airdrome Officer (USAF)

A.O. Army Order

APO Army Post Office

AR Airman Recruit (USN); Army regulations

ARP, A.R.P. Air Raid Precautions (originally British)

ARS Air Rescue Service

arty artillery

AS Apprentice Seaman

A.S.N. Army Service Number

AT Aviation Electronics Technician (USN)

ATC Air Transport Command; Air Traffic Control, formerly

AUS, A.U.S. Army of the United States

AW Articles of War (US Army)

AWOL absent without leave

AWVS American Women's Voluntary Service

BAR Browning automatic rifle

bat battleship (USN)

BBC bromo-benzyl-cyanide (poison gas)

BCD bad conduct discharge

bde brigade

B.E.F. Bonus Expeditionary Force (US History); British Expeditionary Force(s)

bglr bugler

BM Boatswain's Mate (USN)

bn battalion

brev. brevet; brevetted

Brig Brigadier

BT Boilerman (USN)

BTO Big Time Operator, in WW II military slang, a successful braggart; branch transportation Official(s)

btry battery

BU Builder (USN)

bvt. brevet; brevetted

C. Corps

C.A. Coast Artillery (obsolete, but historical)

CAP Civil Air Patrol

cav cavalry

CBI China, Burma, India, a theatre of operations in WW II

CCS Combined Chiefs of Staff, WW II

Cdr. Commander

CE Construction Electrician's Mate (USN); Corps of Engineers

C.G. Coast Guard; Commanding General (historical-obsolete)

CIC Counterintelligence Corps

CINC, C. in C., CinC, C in C, Cinc Commander in Chief

CINCAF, CINCLANT, CINPAC Commander in Chief, Asiatic Fleet; Atlantic (Fleet); Pacific (Fleet) (all USN)

CM court-martial

CMTC, C.M.T.C. Citizen's Military Training Camp

CNO Chief of Naval Operations

CO commanding officer

C of S Chief of Staff

Col. Colonel

Colm. column (Military)

Com. Commander; Commodore

Comdt. Commandant

COMINCH Commander-in-Chief (USN)

COMO, Como. Commodore

CP command post; Construction Apprentice (USN)

Cpl corporal

CPO Chief Petty Officer

CQ Charge of Quarters

C-ration Emergency ration WW II

CSigO Chief Signal Officer

CW chemical warfare

CWO chief warrant officer

CZ Combat Zone

DA Department of the Army

DATA Defense Air Transportation Administration

DC Damage Controlman (USN)

DE Destroyer Escort

DEW distant early warning (DEWline)

DI drill instructor; drill sergeant

div division (US Army)

DO Defense Order

D-ration see C- and K-rations

DV distinguished visitor (Air Force)

EM enlisted men

ens ensign

ETO European Theatre of Operations

FA Field Artillery

FAdm Fleet Admiral

1st Lt. first lieutenant

1 Sgt. first sergeant

ftn fortification; fortified

FPO fleet post office

FYI For Your Information

G1, G2, G3, G4 Asst. C of S, G-1, Personnel; G-2, Intelligence; G-3, Operations; G-4, Logistics

GCI ground controlled interception (station)

GCR ground controlled radar

GHQ, G.H.Q. General Headquarters

GM Gunner's Mate (USN)

GI Government issue; the nickname for an American foot soldier in WW II, and afterward, for any returning serviceman, as "ex-GI"

GO General Orders (US Army)

GQ, G.Q., g.q. general quarters (Nav.)

GS, G.S. General Staff

gun. gunnery

how howitzer

HQ, H.Q., hq, h.q. headquarters

Hq. Co. Headquarters Company

ICBM intercontinental ballistic missile

IFF identification, friend or foe (radar)

IG Inspector General

INF, inf. infantry

Insp. Gen. Inspector General

IRBM intermediate range ballistic missile

JA Judge Advocate

JO journalist (USN)

Judge Adv. Gen. Judge Advocate General

KP kitchen police, the enlisted men who help the cooks; also, their duty

K-ration WW II emergency ration; see C- and D-ration

LC- landing craft (with type specified by following letter, for example, LCI, Landing Craft Infantry

LS- landing ship (of specified type), for example, LST, landing ship, tank

Lt Lieutenant

Lt Col lieutenant colonel

Lt Com lieutenant commander

Lt Gen lieutenant general

Lt (jg.) lieutenant (junior grade)

Lt. Infantry light infantry

MAAG Military Assistance Advisory Group

Maj Major

Maj Gen Major General

MATS Military Air Transport Service

MC, M.C. Medical Corps

MG machine gun

MIG Mikoyan and Gurevich (R.) Soviet jet airplane

mil, mil. military

MOS military occupational specialty (duty classification by number)

MP military police

MSgt, M/Sgt Master sergeant

MTO Mediterranean Theater of Operations (WW II)

MTP Mobilization Training Program

NATE Naval Air Transport Service

NC Nurse Corps

NG, N.G. National Guard

NWC National War College

OCS Officer Candidate School

OD Officer of the Day; olive drab

OG Officer of the Guard

ONI Office of Naval Intelligence

Ord. Sgt. ordnance sergeant

OTC, O.T.C. Officer in Tactical Command; formerly, Officers' Training Camp, or Corps

P prisoner (military personnel "wear the P" when serving a sentence on their home post or base)

Pfc private first class

plat platoon

PM Provost Marshal

PO petty officer

POW prisoner of war

PRO, P.R.O. public relations officer

PT boat patrol torpedo boat (USN)

Pte. private (Brit.)

Pvt private (US Army)

PX post exchange

QM quartermaster

QMC Quartermaster Corps

RA Regular Army (US)

R.A. Royal Artillery

R.A.A.F. Royal Australian Air Force

RACON radar beacon (US Army)

RAdm Rear Admiral (USN)

R.A.F. Royal Air Force

R.C.A.F. Royal Canadian Air Force

Rct recruit (US Army)

RD Radarman (USN)

R.E. Royal Engineers

R.F.A. Royal Field Artillery

R.F.C. Royal Flying Cross

R.N. Royal Navy

R.N.R. Royal Naval Reserve

R.N.V.R. Royal Naval Volunteer Reserve

R.N.Z.A.F. Royal New Zealand Air Force

ROK Republic of Korea armed forces; by extension, **ROK** for any Korean

ROTC, R.O.T.C. Reserve Officers' Training Corps

S1, S2, S3, S4 S-1, Adjutant; S-2, Intelligence Officer; S-3, Operations and Training Officer; S-4, Supply Officer (US Army)

SA seaman apprentice (USN)

SAG Strategic Air Command

SACEUR Supreme Allied Commander Europe

2nd Lt. second lieutenant (GPO)

S1c seaman, first class (GPO)

SFC sergeant first class

Sgt sergeant

SHAEF Supreme Headquarters, Allied Expeditionary Forces

SHAPE Supreme Headquarters, Allied Powers (Europe)

SN Seaman (USN)

SO sonarman (USN)

SP shore patrol, or police (USN)

Sp3c. specialist, third class (GPO)

SP 4, 5, 6, 7, 8 & 9 Specialists 4, 5, 6, 7, 8, and 9

SPARS Women's Coast Guard Reserves (the abbreviation is based on the Coast Guard motto "Semper Paratus — Always Ready.") This was a truly convoluted attempt to keep up with the WACS and WAVES

sq., Sq. squadron

sqd squad

SR Seaman Recruit (USN)

SSgt staff sergeant

TD tank destroyer WW II; Tradevman (i.e., training devices man) (USN)

TDY temporary duty

T Mort trench mortar

trp troop

TS Top Secret

UM underwater mechanic (USN)

USA United States Army

USAF United States Air Force

USAFI United States Armed Forces Institute

USAR United States Army Reserve

USAREUR United States Army, Europe

USCG United States Coast Guard

USMA United States Military Academy

USMC United States Marine Corps

USN United States Navy

USNA United States Naval Academy

USNG United States National Guard

USNR United States Naval Reserve

USO United States Organizations

U.S.S. United States Ship

VA Veterans' Administration

VAdm Vice Admiral

VC Veterinary Corps

VOL Volunteer Officer (US Army)

WAAC Women's Army Auxiliary Corps (obsolete-historical)

WAAF Women's Auxiliary Air Force (Brit.)

WAAS Women's Auxiliary Army Service (Brit.)

WAC Women's Army Corps; a Wac (U.S.)

WAF Women in the Air Force; a Waf (U.S.)

WAFS Women's Auxiliary Ferrying Squadron (US Army)

WASP Women's Air Force Service Pilots

WAVES Women Accepted for Volunteer Emergency Service; a Wave (USN)

WO warrant officer

WRAC Women's Royal Army Corps (Brit.)

WRAF Women's Royal Air Force (Brit.)

WRENS, W.R.N.S. Women's Royal Naval Service (Brit.)

WVS Woman's Voluntary Service (Brit.)

WWI, WWII World War I, World War II

YMS Motor Minesweeper (USN)

YN Yeoman (USN)

Y3c Yeoman third class (USN)

Z zone (used in combination only, US Army)

ZI Zone of Interior (US Army)

Religious Terms

Even after World War I, which was the first great accelerator of the trend to abbreviations in the present century, the number of terms needed in the religious field remained comparable to those for geography, government, the military and science. But the New Deal, World War II, the UN and the fantastic proliferation of scientific terminology has changed the balance utterly. Indeed, this list would be considerably shorter if it were not for the books of the Bible. O tempera! o mores!

Again, many abbreviations such as **Esd., Esth.** and **Ez.** are listed only because they are still in common usage. Fortunately *Acts* and *Amos* are now commonly spelled out.

Bibliography:
Encyclopedia of Ethics and Religion, ed. by James Hastings
Encyclopedia of Religion, ed. by Vergilius Ferm

Religious Terms

A.A. Augustinians of the Assumption (Assumptionists)

A.B.F.M. American Board of Foreign Missions

A.B.M.U. American Baptist Missionary Union

Abp. Archbishop

A.B.S. American Bible Society

A.C. after Christ

A.C.J. American Council for Judaism

A.D. *anno Domini* (L.) in the year of the Lord

A.H. *anno Hegirae* (L.) in the year of Hegira, or flight of Mohammed

A.H.M.S. American Home Mission Society

A.J.C. American Jewish Committee; American Jewish Conference; American Jewish Congress

A.M. *Ave Maria* (L.) Hail Mary

A & M Ancient and Modern (hymns)

A.M.A. American Missionary Association

A.M.D.G. *ad majorem Dei gloriam* (L.) to the greater glory of God

A.M.E. African Methodist Episcopal

A.M.O.R.C. Ancient Mystical Order Rosae Crucis (The Rosicrucian Order)

Angl. Anglican

Annunc. Annunciation

A.P. Associate Presbyterian

Ap. Apostle

Apoc. Apocalypse; Apocrypha; Apocryphal

A.P.S. American Protestant Society

A.R. Recollect Augustinian Fathers. (Initials of R.C. orders do not always stand for the popular name of the order.)

Archd. Archdeacon

A.R.P. Associated Reform Presbyterian

A.R.V. American Standard Revised Version (of the Bible)

A.S.S.U. American Sunday School Union

A.T.S. American Tract Society

A.U.A. American Unitarian Association

Auth. Ver., A.V. Authorized Version (of the Bible)

B. Bible

Bap., Bapt. Baptist

Bar. Baruch (Biblical)

B.B. B'nai B'rith

B.C. before Christ

B.D. *Baccalaureus Divinitatis* (L.) Bachelor of Divinity

Bel and Dr. Bel and the Dragon (Biblical)

B.F.B.S. British and Foreign Bible Society

Bib. Bible; Biblical

Bibl. Biblical

B.M.V. *Beata Maria Virgo* (L.) Blessed Mary the Virgin

Bp. Bishop

Bp. Suff. Bishop Suffragan

Bro. Brother

B.T., B. Th. *Baccalaureus Theologiae* (L.) Bachelor of Theology

B.U. Baptist Union

C. Catholic; Church

Can. Canon

Cant. Canterbury; Canticles

Cantuar. *Cantuariensis* (L.) of Canterbury

Card. Cardinal

Cath. Cathedral; Catholic

C.B.S. Confraternity of the Blessed Sacrament

C.C. Catholic clergyman

C.C.F. Congregation of the Brothers of Charity

C.E. Church of England; Christian Endeavor

Ch. Chaplain; Church

chap. chaplain

Chr. Christ; Christian; Christopher

Chron. Chronicles

cl. clergyman

C.M. Congregation of the Mission (Vincentians, or Lazarists)

c.m. church missionary

C.M.F. Missionary Sons of the Immaculate Heart of Mary (Claretian Missionaries)

C.M.Mh. Missionaries of Marianhill

C.M.S. Church Missionary Society

Col. Colossians (Biblical)

Cong. Congregational

Conglist. Congregationalist

Congr. Orat. Congregation of the Fathers of the Oratory of St. Philip Neri (Oration Fathers)

Cop., Copt. Coptic

Cor. Corinthians (Biblical)

C.R. Congregation of the Resurrection (Resurrectionist Fathers)

C.S. Christian Science; Christian Scientist

C.S.P. Congregation of St. Paul the Apostle (Paulist Fathers)

C.Y.O. Catholic Youth Organization

D. *Deus* (L.) God; *Dominus* (L.) Lord

D. Bib. Douay Bible

D.D. *Divinitatis Doctor* (L.) Doctor of Divinity

Dea. Deacon

Deut. Deuteronomy (Biblical)

D.F. *Defensor Fidei* (L.) Defender of the Faith

D.R. Dutch Reformed

D.Th., D.Theol. Doctor of Theology

D.V. *Deo volente* (L.) God willing; by God's will; Douay Version

eccl., eccles. ecclesiastic

Eccl., Eccles. Ecclesiastes (Biblical)

Ecclus. Ecclesiasticus (Biblical)

E.C.U. English Church Union

Eph., Ephes. Ephesians (Biblical)

Epiph. Epiphany

Epis., Episc. Episcopalian

E.R.V. English Revised Version (of the Bible)

Esd. Esdras (Biblical

Esth. Esther (Biblical)

E.U. Evangelical Union

E.V. English Version (of the Bible)

Exod. Exodus (Biblical)

Ez., Ezr. Ezra (Biblical

Ezek. Ezekial (Biblical)

F.M.S. Marist Brothers

Fr. Father; **Frater** (L.) brother; Friar

F.S.C. Brothers of the Christian Schools (Christian Brothers)

F.S.C.J. Congregation of the Sons of the Sacred Heart of Jesus

F.W.B. Freewill Baptist

Gal. Galatians (Biblical)

Gen. Genesis (Biblical)

G.P. *Gloria Patri* (L.) Glory to the Father

Hab. Habakkuk (Biblical)

Hag. Haggai (Biblical)

H.C. Holy Communion

Heb. Hebrews (Biblical)

H.H. His Holiness (the Pope)

Hos. Hosea (Biblical)

I.B.S.A. International Bible Students' Association (Jehovah's Witnesses)

IHS symbol or monogram for the Greek word for Jesus

I.H.S. *Iesus Hominum Salvator* (L.) Jesus Savior of Men

I.N.R.I. *Iesus Nazarenus Rex Iudaeorum* (L.) Jesus of Nazareth, King of the Jews

Is., Isa. Isaiah (Biblical)

J. Job; Joel (both Biblical)

Jas. James (Biblical)

Jer. Jeremiah (Biblical)

Jo. Bapt. John the Baptist

Jo. Div. John the Divine

Jo. Evang. John the Evangelist

Jon. Jonah (Biblical)

Josh. Joshua (Biblical)

K.C., K. of C. Knights of Columbus

Lam. Lamentations (Biblical)

L. Div. Licentiate in Divinity

L.D.S. Latter Day Saints, Church of Jesus Christ of (the Mormons)

Lev., Levit, Leviticus (Biblical)

Luth. Lutheran

Macc. Maccabees (Biblical)

Mal. Malachi (Biblical)

Mart. Martyrology

Matt. Matthew (Biblical)

47

M.E. Methodist Episcopal

Meth. Methodist

Mgr. Monseigneur; Monsignor

M.I.C. Marian Fathers

Mic. Micah (Biblical)

Moham. Mohammedan

Monsig. Monsignor

M.P. Methodist Protestant

Msgr. Monsignor

Mt. Rev. Most Reverend

M.W. Most Worshipful; Most Worthy

Nah. Nahum (Biblical)

N.C.W.C. National Catholic Welfare Council

Neh. Nehemiah (Biblical)

New Test. New Testament

N.L.C.A. Norwegian Lutheran Church of America

N.T. New Testament

Num., Numb. Numbers (Biblical)

Obad. Obadiah (Biblical)

O.C.R. Order of Cistercian Reform, or Trappists

O.F.M. Order of Friars Minor (Franciscan)

Old. Test. Old Testament

O.P. Order of Preachers (Dominican)

Ortho. Greek Orthodox

O.S.B. Order of St. Benedict (Benedictine)

O.S.U. Order of St. Ursula (Ursuline)

O.T. Old Testament

P.B. Plymouth Brethren; Primitive Baptist

P.E. Presiding Elder; Protestant Episcopal

Pent. Pentacost

Pet. Peter (Biblical)

Phil. Philippians (Biblical)

Philem. Philemon (Biblical)

P.P. Parish Priest

Pr. Priest

Presb. Presbyterian

Prot. Protestant

Prov. Proverbs (Biblical)

Ps., Psa. Psalms (Biblical)

R. Rabbi; respond or response (Church Service)

Rab. Rabbi; rabbinate

rabb. rabbinical

R.C. Roman Catholic

R.C. Ch. Roman Catholic Church

Rect. Rector; Rectory

Ref. Reformation

Ref. Ch. Reformed Church

Ref. Pres. Reformed Presbyterian

Resurr. Resurrection

Rev. Revelation (Biblical); Reverend

Rev. Ver. Revised Version (of the Bible)

Rom. Romans (Biblical)

Rom. Cath. Roman Catholic

R.R. Right Reverend

R.V. Revised Version

R.W. Right Worshipful; Right Worthy

S. Sabbath; Saint

S.A. Salvation Army

Sab. Sabbath

Sam. Samaritan; Samuel (Biblical)

Saml. Samuel (Biblical)

Script. Scripture; scriptural

S.D.A. Seventh Day Adventists

Sem. Seminary

Sep. Septuagint

S.J. Society of Jesus, the Jesuit Fathers

S. of Sol. Song of Solomon (Biblical)

SS. Sancti (L.) Saints

S.S. Sunday School

St. Saint

Sta. Santa

Ste. Sainte

Suff., Suffr. Suffragan

Sus. Susanna (Biblical)

T. Testament

Test. Testament

Test Rec. *Textus Receptus* (L.) Received Text

theol. theologian; theological; theology

theos. theosophical; theosophy

Thess. Thessalonians

Tim. Timothy (Biblical)

Tit. Titus (Biblical)

Tob. Tobit (Biblical)

Trin. Trinitarian; Trinity

U.B. United Brethren

U.F.C. United Free Church (of Scotland)

U.J.A. United Jewish Appeal

Unit. Unitarian; Unitarianism

Univ. Universalist

U.P. United Presbyterian

V. Venerable; Vicar; Virgin

V.A. Vicar Apostolic

Vat. Vatican

Ven. Venerable

Vic. Vicar; Vicarage

Virg. Virgin

V.Rev. Very Reverend

Vulg. Vulgate (version of the Bible)

V.W. Very Worshipful

W. Warden

W.C. Wesleyan Chapel

W.C.T.U. Women's Christian Temperance Union

Westm. Westminster

Wisd. Wisdom of Solomon (Biblical)

W.P. Worthy Patriarch

X Christ; Christian

Xmas Christmas

Xn Christian

Xnty., Xty Christianity

Xtion Christian

Y YMCA, YMHA, YWCA, YWHA, with "the"

Y.M.C.A. Young Men's Christian Association

Y.M. Cath. A. Young Men's Catholic Association

Y.M.H.A. Young Men's Hebrew Association

Y.P.S.C.E. Young People's Society of Christian Endeavor

Y.W. Young Women's Christian Association, with "the"

Y.W.C.A. Young Women's Christian Association

Y.W.H.A. Young Women's Hebrew Association

Zech. Zechariah (Biblical)

Zeph. Zephaniah (Biblical)

Z.O.A. Zionist Organization of America

Zor. Zoroastrian; Zoroastrianism

Scientific and Technical Terms

As an index of our times, scientific and technical terms form the largest single category in this book, even when some of the military terms which could just as well be listed here have been segregated. Again, if you are doing work in any specialized area of the field, it will be necessary to consult the reference library. The field is so enormous and in such constant flux, that it has seemed advisable not to attempt any brief bibliography at this point. Certainly when the specialists disagree (for example, the American Institute of Chemical Engineers uses **B.t.u.** and the American Society of Mechanical Engineers, **Btu** or **B)**, it is difficult if not impertinent for the lexicographer to offer to arbitrate.

Scientific and Technical Terms

A angstrom unit (Physics); argon (Chem.)

A. absolute (temperature); acre (preferred)

a. acre; acreage; ampere; anode; are(s) (metric system); area

A.A. achievement age (Psychol.)

aa ana (L.) of each (Med.)

a.a. always afloat (shipping); author's alteration

A.A.A.S. American Association for the Advancement of Science

A.A.E. American Association of Engineers

Ab alabamine (Chem.)

ABC atomic, biological and chemical

A-bomb atomic bomb

Ac actinium (Chem.); alto-cumulus (Meteorol.)

A.C. Alternating current (Elec.) also a.c.

acc. acceleration

ACE adrenal cortex extraxt

A.C.S. American Cancer Society; American Chemical Society

ACTH adreno-corticotropic hormone

ACW alternating continuous waves (radio)

A.E.C. Atomic Energy Commission

AF audio frequency; also a.f.

Ag argentum (silver) (Chem.)

a.h. ampere-hour(s)

Al aluminum, or aluminium

alc., alcoh. alcohol

alch., alchem. alchemy

alg. algebra

alt. alteration; alternating; altitude

Am alabamine; americium (Chem.)

AM amplitude modulation

am. ammeter (Elec.)

am amplitude

a.m. ampere-minute

amal., amalg. amalgamated

A.M.I.C.E. Associate Member of the Institution of Civil Engineers

A.M.I.E.E. Associate Member of the Institution of Electrical Engineers

A.M.I.Mech.E. Associate Member of the Institution of Mechanical Engineers

amp ampere; amperage

amp.-hr. ampere-hour

Am.Soc.C.E. American Society of Civil Engineers

Am.Soc.M.E. American Society of Mechanical Engineers

An actinium

A.N. arrival notice (shipping)

anal. analogous; analogy; analysis; analytic

anat. anatomical; anatomy

annot. annotated; annotation

ant. antenna

anthrop., anthropol. anthropological; anthropology

antilog. antilogarithm

A.O.S.E. American Order of Stationary Engineers

a.p. author's proof

API American Petroleum Institute

A.P.S. American Physical Society

Ar argon (Chem.)

Ar. *argentum* (L.) silver

a.r. analytical reagent

arch. architect; architecture

archaeol, archeol. archeological; archeology

Arch.E Architectural Engineer

arg. *argentum* (L.) silver

arith. arithmetic; arithmetical

arm. armature

ARPA Advanced Research Projects Agency

A.R.S. American Rocket Society

As alto-stratus (Meteorol.); arsenic (Chem.)

A.S. Academy of Science

as asymmetric (Org. Chem.)

ASA American Standards Association

asb. asbestos

ASCE, A.S.C.E. American Society of Civil Engineers

A.S.M.E. American Society of Mechanical Engineers

ASTM American Society for Testing Materials

astr. astronomer; astronomical; astronomy

astrophys. astrophysical; astrophysics

A.S.W. Association of Scientific Workers

asym. asymmetric; asymmetrical

At astatine (Chem.)

at. airtight; atmosphere; atomic

a.t. ampere turn; assay ton; air temperature

atm. atmosphere; atmospheric

at. no. atomic number

at. vol. atomic volume

at. wt. atomic weight

Au aurum (gold) (Chem.)

A.U. angstrom unit; astronomical unit

auto. automatic; automotive

aux., auxil. auxiliary

av. average; avoirdupois

AVC, a.v.c. automatic volume control (radio)

avdp. avoirdupois

avg. average

avn aviation

avoir. avoirdupois

AW actual weight

A.W.G., AWG American wire gauge

ax. axiom

az. azimuth

B boron (Chem.)

B. Bacillus; Baumé; bearing; bicuspid; breadth

Ba barium (Chem.)

B.A. British Association (for the Advancement of Science)

bact. bacteriology; bacterium

BAL British anti-lewisite

bar. barometer; barrel

B.A.U. British Association Unit

b.b. ball bearing(s)

B.B.C., BBC bromo-benzyl-cyanide (a poison gas)

bbl. barrel; barrels

b.c. bolt circle

BCG (bacillus Calmette-Guérin) anti-tuberculosis vaccine

b/d barrels per day, also b.pd. and bpd

bd. ft. board foot

bds. boards (bookbinding)

Be beryllium (Chem.)

Bess Bessemer

Bev. billion electron volts

bf, b.f. boldface (type)

Bhn Brinell hardness number (A.S.M.E.)

bhp brake horsepower

Bi bismuth (Chem.)

bibliog. bibliographer; bibliography

bicarb. sodium bicarbonate

biochem. biochemistry

biog. biography

biogeog. biogeography

biol. biological; biologist; biology

bitum. bituminous

Bk berkelium (Chem.)

bkbndr. bookbinder

bklr. black letter (Type)

b.m. board measure (lumber); bowel movement (medicine) (baby talk)

B.M.J. British Medical Journal

BMR, b.m.r. basal metabolic rate

bnd. bound

bndg. binding

bot. botanical; botanist; botany

B.P. British Pharmacopoeia

b.p. boiling point

Br bromine (Chem.)

br. bronze

brev. brevier (Type)

B & S Brown and Sharpe gauge

btk buttock

btl. bottle

B.t.u. British thermal unit (usage of A.I.C.E.) Also **B.T.U., B.Th.U., b.t.u., Btu, btu,** and **B**

Bu Butyl (Chem.)

bu. bushel(s)

buck. buckram

bx. box

Bz. benzene

C carbon (Chem.)

C. Celsius; Centigrade; Centimeter

c. candle; capacity (Elec.); carat; cathode; cubic; current

Ca calcium (Chem.)

CA chronological age (Psychol.)

ca. cathode; centiare

Cal. large calorie

cal. calendar; caliber; calorie(s)

c. and s.c. caps and small caps (Printing)

cap. capacity; capitulum

caps. capital letters; capsule

car. carat(s) (preferred)

Cb columbium (Chem.)

CB cast brass

CC cast copper

Cc cirro-cumulus (Meteor.)

cc. cubic centimeters

Cd cadmium (Chem.)

cd. canned; cord

cd. ft. cord foot (feet)

Ce cerium (Chem.)

CE commutator end

c.e. compass error

Cels. Celsius (temperature)

cem. cement

cemf. counter electromotive force

cent. *centum* (L.) one hundred

cent. centered; centigrade; centimeter

ceram. ceramics

Cf californium (Chem.)

cf. calf (binding)

c.f.m., cfm cubic feet per minute

c.g. center of gravity

cg., cg centigram(s)

C.G.S., c.g.s., cgs centimeter-gram-second (system)

CH casehardened

c.h. candle hours

chem. chemical; chemist; chemistry

Ci cirrus (Meteor.)

CI cast iron

cir., circ. circuit; circular; circulation; circumference

cit. citrate

ck. cask

ckw. clockwise

Cl chlorine (Chem.)

CL center line

cl. centiliter(s); cloth

Clar. Clarendon (type)

Cm curium (Chem.)

c.m., cm centimeter; circular mil (wire measure)

Cn cumulo-nimbu (Meteor.)

CN compass north

C.N.S., CNS central nervous system (Med.)

Co cobalt (Chem.)

conch. conchology

cond. conductivity; conductor

conelrad control of electromagnetic radiation (civil defense)

cong. *congius* (L.) gallon

cos cosine

cosec cosecant

cot cotangent

cp candlepower

c.p. chemically pure

cpd. compound

c.p.m. cycles per minute

Cr chromium (Chem.)

craniol craniology

CRP C-reactive protein

cryst. crystallized; crystalline; crystallography

Cs cesium (Chem.); cirro-stratus (Meteor.)

csc cosecant

csk. cask

ctn. cotangent

Cu cumulus (Meteor.); cuprum (copper) (Chem.)

cu. cubic. See **cu. ft., cu. cm., cu. in.**

cur. current

CW continuous wave

cwt. hundredweight

cyclo. cyclotron

cyl. cylinder; cylindrical

D deuterium (Chem.)

D., d. *da* (L.) give (Pharm.); density (Physics); diameter; dose

d. dyne

d. dextro (Chem.)

dal., dal decaliter

db decibel

d.b.h. diameter at breast height (Forestry)

DC, D.C., d.c. direct current

DDT dichlorodiphenyltrichloro-ethane

dec., decim. decimeter

deg. degree(s)

dg. decigram

Di didymium (Chem.)

di., dia., diam. diameter

dkg. dekagram

dkl. dekaliter

dkm. dekameter

dl deciliter

dm. decimeter

doz. dozen

DP, D.P. degree of polymerization; diametrical pitch

dr. dram(s)

d.t. delirium tremens; almost always used as if a plural, "the d.t.'s"

d.w.t. deadweight tons

dwt. denarius weight, i.e., pennyweight

DX, D.X. distance (Radio)

Dy dysprosium (Chem.)

dyn., dynam. dynamics

dz. dozen

E. Earth

e. engineer; engineering; erg

E.A., EA educational age (Psychol.)

Eb erbium (Chem.)

ecol. ecological; ecology

econ. economics

E.E. Electrical Engineer

EEE eastern equine encephalitis

EEG electroencephalogram

EHF extremely high frequency

EKG electrocardiogram

elec., elect. electric; electrical; electrician; electricity

elem. element(s)

embryol. embryology

e.m.f. electromotive force

e.m.u. electromagnetic unit(s)

entom. entomology

EQ educational quotient

eq. equal; equalizer; equalizing; equation; equivalent

equiv. equivalent

Er erbium (Chem.)

ESP extrasensory perception

e.s.u. electrostatic unit(s)

ethnol. ethnology

etym., etymol. etymological; etymology

Eu europium (Chem.)

F Fahrenheit; farad; fathom; fluorine (Chem.); function (Math.)

F. Fahrenheit

f. farad; fathom; fluid (ounce), folio; frequency

f.c. follow copy (Print.)

fcp. foolscap

Fe ferrum (iron) (Chem.)

fir. firkin

Fl fluorine (Chem.)

FM frequency modulation

fm. fathom

fol. folio

F.P., f.p. foot-pound; freezing point

FPIS forward propagation ionospheric scatter

f.p.m. feet per minute

f.p.s. feet per second; frames per second

Fr francium (Chem.)

FSH follicle-stimulating hormone

ft foot

ft. b.m. foot board measure

ft.-c. footcandle

fthm. fathom

ft.-l. foot lambert

ft.-lb. foot-pound

f.v. *folio verso* (L.) on the back of the page

f.w. fresh water

G. specific gravity

G., g. conductance (Elec.); gauge; grain; gram

g general intelligence (Psychol.)

Ga gallium (Chem.)

G.A., g.a. general average

Gal. Galen

gal., gall. gallon(s)

gals. gallons

glv. galvanic

G.C.D., g.c.d. greatest common divisor

Gd gadolinium (Chem.)

Ge germanium (Chem.)

g.e. gilt edges (Bookbinding)

gen. gender; genitive; genus

geneal. genealogy

geod. geodesy; geodetic

geog. geographer; geographic; geographical; geography

geol. geologic; geological; geologist; geology

geom. geometer; geometric; geometrical; geometry

GG gamma globulin (Med.)

GHA Greenwich hour angle (Navigation)

gi. gill(s)

Gl glucinium or glucinum (Chem.)

gloss. glossary

gm. gram(s)

G.M. & S. general, medical, and surgical

G.P. general paresis (Med.)

GPM, g.p.m. gpm gallons per minute

g.p.s. gallons per second

gr. grain(s); gram(s); gross

gro. gross

gr. wt. gross weight

gynecol. gynecological; gynecology

H henry (Elec.); hydrogen (h2 deutorum) (Chem.); intensity of magnetic field (Physics)

H., h. harness; height; high; hour

h. henry (Elec.)

ha. hectare (s)

Hal. halogen (Chem.)

Hb hemoglobin

hcf, h.c.f. highest common factor

He helium (Chem.)

her. heraldry

HF (Preferred), **H.F., h.f.** high frequency

Hf hafnium (Chem.)

hf. bd. half-bound

hf. cf. half-calf

hf. mor. half-morocco

Hg hydrargyrum (mercury) (Chem.)

hg. hectogram; heliogram

hhd. hogshead

hl. hectoliter

hm. hectometer

Ho holmium (Chem.)

hor. horizon; horizontal

horol. horology

hort. horticultural; horticulture

HP, H.P., hp, h.p., hp. high-powered; horsepower

hr. hour(s)

hrs. hours

ht. height; heat

hyd., hydros. hydrostatics

hydraul. hydraulics. Also **hyd.**

Hypo hyposulphite of soda (photography)

hypoth. hypothesis. Also **hyp.**

I iodine (Chem.)

IAEA International Atomic Energy Agency

IAS indicated air speed (Aviation)

ichth. ichthyology

ID, I.D., i.d. inside diameter

IF, I.F., i.f., i-f (**IF** preferred) intermediate frequency

ign. ignition

I.G.Y. International Geophysical Year (July 1957-December 1958)

IHP, I.H.P., ihp, i.h.p., i. hp. indicated horsepower

Il ilinium (Chem.)

ILS instrument landing system (Aviation)

Immunol. immunology

imp. gal. imperial gallon

In indium (Chem.)

in. inch

in.-lb. inch pound

ins. inches; insulated

Io ionium (Chem.)

IQ, I.Q. intelligence quotient

Ir iridium (Chem.)

ital. italic (Type)

IU, I.U. international unit(s) (Biol., Immunol.) measuring amount and effect of a vitamin

J joule (Physics) GPO prefers **j.**

jato jet-assisted takeoff

K cumulus (Meteorol.); *kalium* (L.) potassium

K. Kelvin

K., k. kilogram

k kilo-(thousand)

k. capacity (Elec.); carat (Assaying); constant

ka. kathode or cathode

kc, kc. kilocycle(s)

kcal. kilocalorie

kev. kilo electron volts

kg, kg. keg(s)

kg. kilogram

kil. kilometer(s)

kilo. kilogram; kilometer

kilog. kilogram

kilol. kiloliter

kilom. kilometer

kl., kl kiloliter

km., km kilometer

Kr krypton (Chem.)

kt. carat; kiloton

kv. kilovolt

kv.-a kilovolt-ampere

kw. kilowatt

kw.-hr. (preferred), **K.W.H., kw-h, kw-hr** kilowatt-hour

L length (Physics); terrestrial longitude (Geod.); lambert (Physics)

L, l coefficient of inductance (Elec.)

L. Linnaeus (Botany)

L., l. latitude; length

l. liter

l-, l. levo-. (Chem.)

La lanthanum (Chem.)

lab. laboratory

lat. latitude

lb. libra, *librae* (L.) pound, pounds

lb. ap. pound, apothecary's

lb. av. pound avoirdupois

lbs. pounds

lb. t. pound troy

l.c. left center; lower case (Typog.)

lea. leather

lexicog. lexicographer; lexicographical; lexicography

LF (preferred), **L.F., l.f., lf** low-frequency

lf. lightface (Typog.)

LH luteinizing hormone

LH, L.H., l.h. left hand

Li lithium (Chem.)

li link (chain measure)

lin. lineal; linear

ling. linguistics

liq. liquid; liquor

lith., litho., lithog. lithograph; lithography

log logarithm

long., lon. longitude

loran long-range navigation

lox liquid oxygen

LPG liquefied petroleum gas

L-P long playing

l.t. long ton

Lu lutecium (Chem.)

l.w.l. load waterline

l.w.m. low watermark

M., m. manual; mass; medicine: medium; meridian; *meridies* (L.) noon; mile; mill; minim; minute; modulus; month

m., m meter

MA, M.A. mental age (Psychol.)

Ma masurium (Chem.)

ma. milliampere (Elec.)

m.a.f. moisture and ash free (coal)

mag. magnitude (of a star)

math. mathematical; mathematician; mathematics

M b.m. thousand (feet) board measure

mc, mc., m.c. megacycle. Also **meg.**

M c.f. one thousand cubic feet

Me methyl (Chem.)

m.e. marbled edges (Books)

meas. measure

mech. mechanical; mechanics

meg. megacycle

meq. milliequivalent

mer. meridian; meridional

metal. metallurgy

meteorol. meteorology

Mev., Mev, mev, m.è.v. million electron volts

mf milli-fard

Mg magnesium (Chem.)

mG milligauss

mg. (preferred), **mg, mgm** milligram(s)

mh. millihenry

mi. mile; mill

micros. microscopy

min. mineralogical; mineralogy; minim; maximum; mining; minute(s)

mineral. mineralogy

mks, m.k.s. meter-kilogram-second (system)

ml. milliliter

mm., mm millimeter(s); *millia* (L.) thousands

m.m.f. magnetomotive force (Engineering)

mmfd. micromicrofarad
Mn manganese (Chem.)

Mo molybdenum (Chem.)

mol. wt. molecular weight

mor. morocco (Bookbinding)

morphol morphology

m.p. melting point

m.p.h., mph miles per hour

msec. millisecond

m.s.l. mean sea level

Ms-Th mesothorium (Chem.)

mt. megaton

m.t. metric ton

mya. myriare

mycol. mycology

myg. myriagram

myl. myrialiter

mym. myriameter

N nitrogen (Chem.)

N normal

N., n. normal (strength solution) (Chem.)

Na *natrium* (L.) sodium (Chem.)

Nb niobium (Chem.)

N.C., n.c. nitrocellulose

Nd neodymium (Chem.)

Ne neon (Chem.)

N.F. National Formulary (Pharm.)

n.f.e. non-ferrous extract

Ni nickel (Chem.)

n.l. natural log or logarithm; new line (Print.)

NP neuropsychiatric

Np neptunium (Chem.)

n.p. no paging (of books); no place (of publication of books)

NPN, N.P.N. nonprotein nitrogen

n.p. or d. no place or date (books)

n.p.t. normal pressure and temperature

Ns nimbo-stratus

Nt nitron (Chem.)

nt. weight. net weight

O oxygen (Chem.)

o ohm

o- ortho. (Chem.)

o. *octarius* (L.) pint (Pharm.)

org. organic

ornith., ornithol. ornithological; ornithology

oz. ounce(s)

oz. ap. ounce (apothecaries' weight)

oz. av. ounce (avoirdupois)

ozs. ounces

oz. t. ounce troy

P parental (Biol.); phosphorous (Chem.); pressure (Phys.)

p. perch (the measure); pint; pole (the measure); population

p- para- (Chem.)

Pa protoactinium (Chem.)

PABA, paba para-aminobenzoic acid

paleol. paleology

paleon. paleontology

path., pathol. pathology

Pb *plumbum* (L.) lead (Chem.)

P.B. *Pharmacopoeia Britannica* (L.) British Pharmacopoeia

Pd palladium (Chem.)

P.E. probable error (Statistics)

petrog. petrography

petrol. petrology

pF water energy (**p.** logarithm; **F.** frequency)

pH hydrogen-ion concentration

Ph phenyl (Chem.)

Pharm., Phar. pharmaceutical; pharmacopoeia; pharmacy

phys. physical; physician; physics

physiol. physiological; physiology

Po polonium (Chem.)

PP pellagra preventative (factor)

Pr praseodymium (Chem.)

p.s.f., psf pounds per square foot

p.s.i., psi pounds per square inch

Pt platinum (Chem.)

pt. part; pint

Pu plutonium (Chem.)

pwt. pennyweight

Q., q. quarto, Plural **Qq**

q. quart; quarter (of a hundredweight); quintal; quire

Q.F. quick-firing

ql. quintal

Qq quartos

qr. quarter; quire

qt. quantity; quart(s)

qto. quarto

R radical, esp. hydrocarbon radical (Chem.); radius; ratio (Math.) gas constant (Phys. Chem.)

R, r resistance (Elec.)

R. Reaumur; ring (Org. Chem.)

r roentgen(s)

Ra radium (Chem.)

R.A. right ascension (Astron.)

racon radar beacon

rad. radical; radix

radar radio detection and ranging

rato rocket-assisted takeoff

Rb rubidium (Chem.)

rd. rod; round

Réaum. Réaumur

r.e.p. roentgen equivalent physical

RF radiofrequency

R.F., r.f. radio frequency; rapid-fire

Rh Rhesus (blood factor); rhodium (Chem.)

r.h. relative humidity

rheo. rheostat(s)

rm. ream (Paper)

rms., r.m.s. root mean square

Rn radon (Chem.)

ROP run of paper

rpm, r.p.m. revolutions per minute

rps., r.p.s. revolutions per second

R.Q. respiratory quotient

Ru ruthenium (Chem.)

Rx. recipe

S sulfur (Chem.)

s. sacaral (Anatomy)

s- symmetrical (Chem.)

Sa samarium (Chem.)

s.ap. scruple (apothecaries' weight)

Sb *stibium* (L.) antimony

Sc scandium (Chem.); strato-cumulus (Meteor.)

scr. scruple

S.D., s.d. standard deviation (Statistics)

Se selenium (Chem.)

sec secant (Geom., Trig.)

sec.-ft. second-foot

sech hyperbolic secant

secs. seconds; sections

sect. section (Measure.; Biol.; Micros.)

seismol. seismology

sep. sepal (Bot.)

Sf. Svedberg flotation

s.g. specific gravity

SHA sidereal hour angle (Navigation)

SHF superhigh frequency

shoran short range (radio)

s. hp. shaft horsepower

Si silicon (Chem.)

sinh hyperbolic sine

S. lat. south latitude

Sm samarium (Chem.)

Sn stannum (Chem.)

sofar sound fixing and ranging

sol. soluble; solution

sonar sound navigation and ranging

spec. specification

sp. gr. specific gravity

sp. ht. specific heat

spp. species (plural)

sq. square; in compounds, as sq. ft., sq. in., etc.

Sr strontium (Chem.)

S.S.F. standard Saybolt furol

S.S.U. standard Saybolt universal

St stratus

st. stere

s.t. short ton

sta. stator (Mach.)

stat. statute (miles)

std. c.f. standard cubic foot (feet)

ster., stg. sterling

surv. survey; surveying; surveyor

sym-, sym. symmetrical (Chem.)

T tantalum (Chem.); temperature (on the absolute scale); (surface) tension; tritium

t. temperature; ton, or tons; tonneau (F.) (metric) ton; troy(wt.)

T- triple bond (Chem.)

Ta tantalum (Chem.)

tan, tan. tangent

tanh hyperbolic tangent

Tb terbium (Chem.)

t.b. trial balance

Tc technetium

tc. tierce; tierces

T.D.N., t.d.n. totally digestible nutrients

Te tellurium (Chem.)

temp. temperature

Th thorium (Chem.)

Th-Em thoron (Chem.)

theor. theorem

therm. thermometer

Ti titanium (Chem.)

tinct. tincture (Pharm.)

Tl thallium

t.m. true mean

Tm thulium (Chem.)

Tn thoron (Chem.)

tn. ton

TNT, T.N.T. trinitrotoluene; trinitrotoluol

top. topographical

topog. topography; -ical

tox., toxicol. toxicology

Tr terbium (Chem.)

trans. transpose (Alg.); transverse (Geom.)

t.r.f., t-r-f, T.R.F. tuned radio frequency

trig., trigon. trigonometrical; trigonometry

trit. triturate (Pharm.)

Tu thulium; tungsten

2,4-D insecticide

U uranium (Chem.)

UHF, U.H.F., u.h.f. ultra-high frequency

Ur uranium (Chem.)

u.t. universal time

V vanadium (Chem.)

V, v volt; volume

v. valve; ventral; volt; voltage; volume

VAR visual-aural range

var. variant; variation; variometer

Vd vanadium (Chem.)

VHF, V.H.F., v.h.f. very high frequency

Vi virginium (Chem.)

VLF very low frequency

W, w watt

W wolfram (G.) tungsten (Chem.)

W., w. weight; width; work (Physics)

watt-hr. watt-hour

w.-hr. watt-hour

WL, w.l. wave length

W. long. west longitude

wt. weight

x an abscissa (Geom.); an unknown quantity (Math.)

Xe xenon (Chem.)

Y yttrium (Chem.)

y an unknown quantity (Math.)

Yb ytterbium (Chem.)

Yt yttrium (Chem.)

Z atomic number (Chem.); zenith distance (Astron.)

z an unknown quantity (Math.)

z. zero

Zn zinc (Chem.)

zooph. zoophytology

Zr zirconium (Chem.)

General Index

A

A angstrom unit (Physics); argon (Chem.) N.B.: The period, or point, is never used with the symbol for chemical elements; army (Mil.)

A. absolute (Temperature); Academician; Academy; acre (preferred); alto (Music); America; American; answer

a. about; accepted (Com.); acre; acreage; acting; adjective; after; afternoon; amateur; ampere; *anno* (L.) in the year; anode; anonymous; *ante* (L.) before; approved (Com.); are(s) (Metric System); area; argent (Her.)

AA achievement age (Psychol.); Airman Apprentice (USN); antiaircraft (Mil.)

A.A. Alcoholics Anonymous; Associate in Arts; Augustinians of the Assumption (Assumptionists)

a.a. *ana* (L) of each (Med.)

a.a. author's alteration

AAA Agricultural Adjustment Agency (or Act, or Administration)

A.A.A. Amateur Athletic Association; Automobile Association of America

AAAA American Association of Advertising Agencies; also known as 4A

A.A.A.A. Amateur Athletic Association of America

A.A.A.L. American Academy of Arts and Letters

A.A.A.S. American Association for the Advancement of Science

AACS US Airforce Airways and Air Communications Service, formerly, Army Air Communications System

A.A.E. American Association of Engineers

A. & M. Agricultural and Mechanical (cf. Texas A. & M.)

A. and M. Ancient and Modern (hymns)

A.A.P.S.S. American Academy of Political and Social Science

A.A.U. Amateur Athletic Union

A.A.U.P. American Association of University Professors

A.A.U.W. American Association of University Women

Ab alabamine (Chem.)

A.B. able-bodied seaman; *Artium Baccalaureus* (L.) Bachelor of Arts

ABA American Booksellers Association

A.B.A. American Bar Association

A.B.A.J. American Bar Association Journal

abbr., abbrev. abbreviated; abbreviation

ABC American Broadcasting Company; atomic, biological and chemical

abd. abdicated

Aber. Aberdeen (Scotland)

A.B.F.M. American Board of Foreign Missions

ab. init. *ab initio* (L.) from the beginning

abl. ablative

abn airborne

abo. aboriginal

A-bomb atomic bomb

Abp. Archbishop

abr. abridged; abridgement

A.B.S. American Bible Society; American Bureau of Shipping

abs. absent; absolute; absolutely; abstract

abstr. abstract; abstracted

abt. about

abv. above

Ac actinium (Chem.); alto-cumulus (Meteorol.)

AC Air Controlman (USN)

A.C. Alternating current (Elec.); Athletic Club, as in N.Y.A.C.

A/C, A.C. account current (Banking)

a/c, acct. account

a.c. alternating current

acad. academic; academy

ACC Air Co-ordinating Committee

acc. acceleration; according; account; accusative

Acce., Acpt. acceptance (Banking)

accel. *accelerando* (Mus.)

accrd. int. accrued interest

acct. account; accountant

accum. accumulative

A.C.D. American College of Dentists

ACE adrenal cortex extract

A.C.J. American Council for Judaism

ack. acknowledge; acknowledgement

A.C.L.S. American Council of Learned Societies

A.C.L.U. American Civil Liberties Union

ACofS Assistant Chief of Staff (US Army)

A.C.P. American College of Physicians

acpt. acceptance (Banking)

A.C.S. American Cancer Society; American Chemical Society; American College of Surgeons; American Colonization Society

A/cs pay. accounts payable

A/cs rec. accounts receivable

act. active (voice) (Grammatical)

actg. acting

ACTH adreno-corticotropic-hormone, a drug useful in treating arthritis (1951)

ACW alternating continuous waves (radio)

A.C.W.A. Amalgamated Clothing Workers of America

A.D. *anno Domini* (L.) in the year of our Lord

ad advertisement

a.d. after date

A.D.A. American Dental Association; Americans for Democratic Action

A.D.C., ADC, a.d.c. aide-de-camp

add. addenda; addendum; addition; additional; address

ad infin. *ad infinitum* (L.) to infinity

ad init. *ad initium* (L.) to or at the beginning

ad int. *ad interim* (L.) in the meantime

adj. adjacent; adjective; adjoining; adjourned; adjudged; adjunct; adjustment (Banking); adjutant

Adj. Gen. Adjutant General (GPO)

ADL Anti-Defamation League (of B'nai B'rith)

ad lib *ad libitum* (L.) at pleasure

Adm. Admiral; Admiralty; Administrator; Administration

adm. administrator; administration; administrative; admission

admx., adm(tr)x. administratrix

adrm. airdrome

a.d.s. autograph document signed

A.D.S. American Dialect Society

Adv. Advent; Advocate

adv. ad valorem; advance; adverb; adverbial; adverbially; adversus; advertisement

ad. val. *ad valorem* (L.) according to value

adv. chgs. advance charges

adv. frt. advanced freight

advt. advertisement

AE account executive (Bus.)

AE pen name of George Russell, Irish author

A.E.A. Actor's Equity Association; American Economic Association

A.E. and P. Ambassador Extraordinary and Plenipotentiary

A.E.C. Atomic Energy Commission

A.E.F. American Expeditionary Force or Forces

aet., aetat. *aetatis* (L.) aged; of age

AF Air Force (USAF); audio frequency; Aviation Photographer's Mate (USN)

AF. Anglo-French

A.F. army form

Af. Africa; African; Afrikaans (South African Dutch)

a.f. audio frequency

A.F.A.M., A.F. & A.M. Ancient Free and Accepted Masons

AFB Air Force Base (USAF)

A.F.B. American Foundation for the Blind

Afg. Afghanistan

A1c airman, first class

AFL, A.F. of L. American Federation of Labor

AFL-CIO, A.F. of L.-C.I.O. combined American Federation of Labor and Congress of Industrial Organizations

A.F.M. American Federation of Musicians

Afr. Africa; African

AFRA, A.F.R.A. American Federation of Radio Artists

A.F.S. American Field Service

A.A.S.F. African American Students Foundation

A.F.T. American Federation of Teachers

AFTRA American Federation of Television and Radio Artists

aft. afternoon

AFUS Air Force of the United States (US Army)

Ag argentum (silver) (Chem.)

AG Adjutant General (Mil.); Aerographer's Mate (USN)

A.G. Attorney General; Author's Guild; *Aktiengesellschaft* (German joint-stock company)

Ag. August

a.g.b. any good brand

AGC Adjutant General's Corps (Mil.)

AGCT Army General Classification Test

agcy. agency

Agfa German photographic company (*Aktiengesellschaft fur anilinfabrication*)

agn. again

agr., agri., agric. agricultural, agriculture, agriculturist

AGS Army General Staff

agst. against

agt. agent; agreement

Agua. Aguascalientes (Mexico)

AGVA, A.G.V.A. American Guild of Variety Artists

A.H. *anno Hegirae* (L.) in the year of Hegira, or flight of Mohammed

a.h. ampere-hour(s)

a. & h. accident and health (insurance)

A.H.A. American Historical Association; American Hospital Association

A.H.C.P. Arab High Committee on Palestine

A.H.M.S. American Home Mission Society

AHQ Army Headquarters

A.I.A. American Institute of Architects

A.I.D. American Institute of Decorators

A.J. Associate Justice

A.J.C. American Jewish Committee; American Jewish Conference; American Jewish Congress

A.J.I.L. American Journal of International Law

AK Aviation Storekeeper (USN)

a.k.a. also known as

A.K.C. American Kennel Club; Associate of King's College (London)

AL Aviation Electronicsman (USN)

Al aluminum, or aluminium (chem).

AL. Anglo-Latin

A.L. American League (baseball); American Legion

a.l. autograph letter

Ala. Alabama

A.L.A., ALA American Library Association; Authors League of America; Automobile Legal Association

Alas. Alaska

Alb. Albania; Albanian; Albany; Albert; Alberta (Canada)

Alba. Alberta (Canada)

alc., alcoh. alcohol

alch., alchem. alchemy

Alcoa, ALCOA Aluminum Company of America

Ald., Aldm. Alderman

Alex. Alexander; Alexandra

Alf. Alfonso; Alfred

Alg. Algeria; Algernon

alg. algebra

ALITALIA *Aerolinee Italiane Internazionali*

all' ott. *all' ottava* (It.) an octave higher than written

A.L.P. American Labor Party

A.L.R. American Law Reports

a.l.s. autograph letter signed

alt. alteration; alternate; alternating; alternations; alternative; altitude; alto (Music)

Alta. Alberta (Canada)

alum. aluminum; alumnus

Am alabamine; americium

A.M., AM, a.m. *ante meridiem* (L.) before noon

A.M. *Artium Magister* (L.) Master of Arts; *Ave Maria* (L.) Hail Mary

AM amplitude modulation; Aviation Structural Mechanic (USN)

Am. America; American; Americanism

am amplitude

am. ammeter (Elec.)

a.m. ampere-minute

A/M *Am Mainz* (G.) on the Mainz River

A.M.A. American Management Association; American Medical Association; American Missionary Association

amal., amalg. amalgamated

Amb. Ambassador; ambulance

A.M.C. American Maritime Cases

Am. Dec. American Decisions (legal)

A.M.D.G. *ad majorem Dei gloriam* (L.) to the greater glory of God

amdt. amendment

A.M.E. African Methodist Episcopal

AMEDS Army Medical Service

Amer. America; American

Amer. G.S. American Geographical Society

AMG, A.M.G., Amgot Allied, also American, Military Government (of Occupied Territory)

A.M.I.C.E. Associate Member of the Institution of Civil Engineers

A.M.I.E.E. Associate Member of the Institution of Electrical Engineers

A.M.I.Mech.E. Associate Member of the Institution of Mechanical Engineers

Am. Ind. American Indian (language)

ammo ammunition (US Army)

A.M.O.R.C. Ancient Mystical Order Roses Crucis (The Rosicrucian Order)

amp. ampere; amperage

amp.-hr. ampere-hour

A.M.P.A.S. Academy of Motion Picture Arts and Sciences

Am. Rep. American Reports (legal)

Am. Soc. C.E. American Society of Civil Engineers

Am.Soc.M.E. American Society of Mechanical Engineers

Amst. Amsterdam

Am. St. Paps. American State Papers (legal)

Am. St. Rept. American State Reports (legal)

amt. amount

Amtorg *Amerikanskaya torglovya* (Russ.) Russian Trading Corporation

AMTRAC amphibious tractor (US Army)

AMVETS American Veterans (of World War II)

An actinon (Chem.)

AN Airman (USN)

A.N. Anglo-Norman; arrival notice (Shipping)

anal. analogous; analogy; analysis; analytic

anat. anatomical; anatomy

A.N.C. American News Company; Army Nurse Corps

anc. ancient

And. Andorra

and. *andante* (Music)

ANG Air National Guard

A.N.G., ANG American Newspaper Guild (AFL-CIO)

Ang. Anglesey (Wales)

Angl. Anglican

anim. *animato* (Music)

ann. *anni* (L.) years, annual; annuity

anniv. anniversary

annot. annotated; annotation; annotator

Ann. Rep., ann. rep. annual report

Annunc. Annunciation

Anon., anon. anonymous

A.N.P.A., ANPA American Newspaper Publishers Association

ans. answer; answered

Ant. Antarctica; Anthony; Antrim (Ireland)

ant. antenna; antiquarian; antique; antonym

ANTA American National Theatre and Academy

Ant. & Cl. Antony and Cleopatra (Shakespeare) Note: Hereafter, abbreviated to Shak.

anthol. anthology

anthrop., anthropol. anthropological; anthropology

antilog antilogarithm

antiq. antiquarian; antiquities

ANZAC, Anzac Australian and New Zealand Army Corps

AO Aviation Ordnanceman (USN)

A.O. Army Order

A/o account of

A.O.F. Ancient Order of Foresters

A.O.H. Ancient Order of Hibernians

A1 first class

aor. aorist (Gram.)

a/or, &/or, and/or either *and* or *or*

A.O.S.E. American Order of Stationary Engineers

AP airplane (Mil.); antipersonnel; armorpiercing

AP, A.P. Associated Press

A.P. Associate Presbyterian

A/P authority to pay, or purchase

Ap. Apostle; April

A & P The Great Atlantic and Pacific Tea Company

a.p. additional premium; assessment paid; author's proof

A.P.A. American Philological Association; American Protective Association; American Psychiatric Association

API American Petroleum Institute

APO Army Post Office

apog. apogee

Apoc. Apocalypse; Apocrypha; Apocryphal

App. Appellate

app. apparatus; apparent; apparently; appended; appendix; applied; appointed; apprentice; approved; approximate

appar. apparent; apparently

appd. approved

App. D.C. District of Columbia Appeals (legal)

appmt. appointment

APPR Army package power reactor

Apr. April

A.P.S. American Peace Society; American Philosophical Society; American Physical Society; American Protestant Society

A.P.S.A. American Political Science Association

apt., apts. apartment; apartments

apx. appendix

A.Q., AQ achievement (accomplishment or attainment) quotient

aq *aqua* (L.) water

Ar argon (Chem.)

AR Airman Recruit (USN); Army; Army Regulation(s)

A.R. Recollect Augustinian Fathers; Annual Return

Ar. Arabian; Arabic; Aramaic; *argentum* (L.) silver

ar. argent (Her.); aromatic; arrival; arrive; arrives

a.r. all rail; all risks (Insurance); analytical reagent

ARA Agricultural Research Administration

A.R.A. American Railway Association; Associate of the Royal Academy

Arab. Arabian; Arabic

Aram. Aramaic

Aramco. Arabian American Oil Co.

arbor. arboriculture

arbtrn. arbitration

ARC, A.R.C. American (National) Red Cross

Arch. Archbishop; Archibald

arch. archaic; archaism; archery; archipelago; architect; architecture

archaeol. archaeological; archaeology

Archd. Archdeacon; Archduke

Arch.E. Architectural Engineer

archeol. archeological; archeology

archit. architecture

archt. architect

Arg. Agentina; Argentine; Argyll

arg. argent (Her.); *argentum* (L.) silver

arith. arithmetic; arithmetical

Ariz. Arizona

Ark. Arkansas

Arm. Armagh (Ireland); Armenian; Armoric

arm. armature

Ar. M. Master of Architecture

Armen. Armenian

ARP, A.R.P. Air Raid Precautions (Originally British)

A.R.P. Associated Reform Presbyterian

arp. arpeggio (Music)

ARPA Advanced Research Projects Agency

arr. arranged; arrangements; arrive; arrived

arrgt. arrangement

ARS Air Rescue Service (Mil.)

A.R.S. American Rocket Society

art. article; artificer; artificial; artillery

arty artillery (Mil.)

A.R.U. American Railway Union

A.R.V. American Standard Revised Version (of the Bible)

AS apprentice seaman (USN)

As alto-stratus (Meteorol.); arsenic (Chem.)

AS. Anglo-Saxon

A.S. Academy of Science

As. Asia; Asian; Asiatic

as asymmetric (Org. Chem.)

ASA American Standards Association

asb. asbestos

A.S.C. American Society of Cinematographers

ASCAP, A.S.C.A.P. American Society of Composers, Authors and Publishers

ASCE, A.S.C.E. American Society of Civil Engineers

asgd. assigned

asgmt. assignment

A.S.M.E. American Society of Mechanical Engineers

asmt. assortment

A.S.N. Army service number

A.S.P.C.A. American Society for the Prevention of Cruelty to Animals

ass. assistant; association

assd. assigned

assn. association

assnd. assigned

assoc. associate; association

A.S.S.R. Autonomous Soviet Socialist Republic

asst. assessment; assistant

A.S.S.U. American Sunday School Union

ass'y assembly

ASTM American Society for Testing Materials

Assyr. Assyrian

ASTP Army Specialized Training Program

astr. astronomer; astronomical; astronomy

astrophys. astrophysical; astrophysics

A.S.U. American Students Union

A.S.W. Association of Scientific Workers

asym. asymmetric; asymmetrical

AT Aviation Electronics Technician (USN)

At astatine (Chem.)

A/T American terms (grain trade)

at. airtight; atmosphere; atomic

a.t. ampere turn; assay ton; air temperature; air transport

ATC Air Traffic Control; formerly, Air Transport Command

atdt. attendant

a temp. *a tempo* (Music)

athl. athletics

Atl. Atlantic

Atl. A. Atlantic Reporter (legal)

atm. atmosphere; atmospheric

at. no. atomic number

A.T.S. American Tract Society

ats. at suit of (legal)

Att. Attorney

A. T. & T. American Telephone and Telegraph Co.

att. attach; attache; attached

att., attn., atten. attention

attrib. attribute; attributive; attributively

atty. attorney

Atty. Gen. Attorney General

at. vol. atomic volume

ATW American Theatre Wing

at. wt. atomic weight

Au aurum (gold) (Chem.)

A.U. angstrom unit; astronomical unit

Au. author

A.U.A. American Unitarian Association

A.U.C. *ab urbe condita; anno urbis conditae* (L.) from; in the year of, the founding of the city, i.e. Rome

aud. audit; auditor

Aug. August

AUS, Army of the United States

Aus. Australia

Aust. Austria; Austrian

Austl., Austral. Australia; Australasia

auth. authentic; author; authoress; authorized; authority

Auth. Ver. Authorized Version (of the Bible)

auto. automatic; automotive

aux., auxil. auxiliary

A.V. Authorized Version (of the Bible)

a.v., a/v, A/V *ad valorem* (L.) according to value

Av. Avenue

av. average; avoirdupois

AVC, A.V.C. American Veterans Committee

AVC, a.v.c. automatic volume control (radio)

avdp. avoirdupois

Ave. Avenue

avg. average

avn. aviation

avoir. avoirdupois

AW Articles of War (US Army)

A/W Actual weight; all water (Transp.)

a.w. all water

a/w all weight

A.W.G., AWG American wire gauge

A.W.M. American War Mothers

A.W.O.L., AWOL absent without leave (Mil.)

AWVS American Women's Voluntary Service

ax. axiom

A.Y.D. American Youth for Democracy

A.Y.H. American Youth Hostels

A.Y.L.I. As You Like It (Shak.)

A.Y.M. Ancient York Mason

az. azimuth; azure (Her.)

A.Z.C. American Zionist Council

Az. Is. Azores Islands

Azo. Azores

B

B Bishop (Chess); boron (Chem.)

B. bacillus; Baume; Bible; British; Brotherhood

B., b. bachelor; balboa (mon. unit, Pan.) base; basso (Music); bat; battery; bay; bearing; belga (Belg. mon. unit, until end of WWII); bicuspid; bill; boils; bolivar (Venez. mon. unit); boliviano (Bol. mon. unit); book; born; breadth; brother

B/— bag; bale

Ba barium (Chem.)

B.A. *Baccalaureus Artium* (L.) Bachelor of Arts; British Academy; British Association (for the Advancement of Science); Buenos Aires

Bab. Babylonian

bach. bachelor

bact. bacteriology; bacterium

BAE Bureau of Agricultural Economics; Bureau of American Ethnology

B. Agr. *Baccalaureus Agriculturae* (L.) Bachelor of Agriculture

B. Ag. Sc. Bachelor of Agricultural Science

Ba. Is. Bahama Islands

BAL British anti-lewisite (Mil.)

Bal. Baluchistan

Bal., bal. balance

B. and B. brandy and Benedictine

B. and S. brandy-and-soda

BANK International Bank for Reconstruction and Development

Bap., Bapt. Baptist

bap.; bapt. baptized

BAR Browning automatic rifle

Bar. Baruch (Biblical)

bar. barometer; barrel; barrister

Barb. Barbados; Barbara

B.Arch. Bachelor of Architecture

barit. baritone

barr. barrister

Bart. Baronet; Bartholomew

Bas. Basutoland

bat battle (US Army); battleship (USN)

batt. battery

B.A.U. British Association Unit

Bav. Bavaria; Bavarian

B.B. Blue Book; B'nai B'rith

b.b. bail bond; ball bearing(s); balloon barrage; bank bill; bank; book; baseball; base on balls; bearer bonds; black-bordered; break bulk

B/B, b/g bonded goods

B.B.A. Bachelor of Business Administration

B.B.C., BBC British Broadcasting Corporation

B.B.C., BBC bromo-benzyl-cyanide (a poison gas)

b.b.c. baseball club

BBDO Batten Barton Durstine & Osborn, Inc. (Bus.)

bbl. barrel; barrels

B.B.S. Bachelor of Business Science

B.C. Bachelor of Chemistry; Before Christ; Boston College; British Columbia

B/C bills for collection

b.c. boat club; bolt circle

BCD bad conduct discharge (US Army)

B.C.E. Bachelor of Chemical Engineering; Bachelor of Civil Engineering

BCG (bacillus Calmette-Guérin) anti-tuberculosis vaccine

B.Ch. *Baccalaureus Chirurgiae* (L.) Bachelor of Surgery

bch. bunch

B.C.L. Bachelor of Civil Law

B.D. Bachelor of Divinity; bank draft; bills discounted

B/D bank draft

b.d. back dividends (stocks)

bd. board; bond; bound

b/d barrels per day

bde brigade (Mil.)

bd. ft. board foot

bdl. bundle

B.D.S. Bachelor of Dental Surgery

bds. boards (bookbinding); bonds

BDSA Business and Defense Services Administration

Be beryllium (Chem.)

B.E. Bachelor of Education; Bachelor of Engineering; Board of Education

B/E bill of entry; bill of exchange

BEC Bureau of Employees' Compensation

bec. because

Bech. Bechuanaland

Beds Bedfordshire (England)

B.E.E. Bachelor of Electrical Engineering

B.E.F. Bonus Expeditionary Force (U.S. History) unemployed WW I veterans who marched to Washington, D.C. in 1932; British Expeditionary Forces

bef. before

beg. begin; beginning

bel. below

Bel and Dr. Bel and the Dragon (Biblical)

Belg. Belgian; Belgium

Belg.Cong. Belgian Congo (now Congo Republic, Leopoldville)

B.E.M. British Empire Medal

BENELUX, Benelux Belgium-The Netherlands-Luxemburg

Beng. Bengali

Benj. Benjamin

Ber. Berlin; Bermuda

Ber. Is. Bermuda Islands

Berks Berkshire (England)

Berw. Berwick (Scotland)

B. ès L. *Bachlier ès Lettres* (F.) Bachelor of Letters

B. ès S. Bachelier ès Sciences (F.) Bachelor of Science

Bess. Bessemer (Scientific)

bet., betw. between

Bev. billion electron volts

BEW Board of Economic Warfare

B/F brought forward

B.F. Bachelor of Finance; Bachelor of Forestry

bf, b.f. boldface (type)

bf. brief (legal)

B.F.A. Bachelor of Fine Arts

B.F.B.S. British and Foreign Bible Society

BFDC Bureau of Foreign and Domestic Commerce

B.G. Brigadier General

bg. bag

B-girl bar girl (1948)

bglr bugler (Mil.)

bgs. bags

Bhn Brinell hardness number (A.S.M.E.)

bhp brake horsepower

Bhu. Bhutan

Bi bismuth (Chem.)

Bib. Bible; biblical

Bibl., bibl. biblical; bibliographical

bibliog. bibliographer; bibliography

bicarb. sodium bicarbonate

biochem. biochemistry

biog. biographer; biographical, biography

biogeog. biogeography

biol. biological; biologist; biology

B.I.S. Bank for International Settlements

bitum. bituminous

B.J. Bachelor of Journalism

Bk berkelium (Chem.)

bk. bank; bark; block; book

bkbndr. bookbinder

bkcy. bankruptcy

bkg. banking

bklr. black letter (Type)

bkpg. bookkeeping

bkpr. bookkeeper

bkpt. bankrupt

bks. barracks; books

bkt. basket; bracket

B.L. Bachelor of Laws; Bachelor of Literature

B/L bill of lading

b.l. base line; bill lodged; breech-loading

bl. bale; barrel; black; block; blue

bldg. building

B.L.E. Brotherhood of Locomotive Engineers

B. Lit(t)., B. Lit. *Baccalaureus Lit(t)eratum* (L.) Bachelor of Literature

blk. black; block; bulk

Bln., bln. balloon

BLS Bureau of Labor Statistics

B.L.S. Bachelor of Library Science

bls. bales; barrels

blvd. boulevard

BM Boatswain's Mate (USN)

B.M. Bachelor of Medicine; Bachelor of Music; British Museum

b.m. board measure (Lumber); bowel movement (Medicine)

B & M Boston and Maine Railroad

B. of M. bill of material

B.M.E. Bachelor of Mining Engineering

B. Mech. E. Bachelor of Mechanical Engineering

BMI Broadcast Music Inc.

B.M.J. British Medical Journal

BMR, b.m.r. basal metabolic rate

B.M.V. *Beata Maria Virgo* (L.) Blessed Mary the Virgin

B.Mus. Bachelor of Music

B.N., b.n. bank note

Bn., bn. Baron; battalion

bnd. bound

bndg. binding

B.O. body odor, the abbrev. being a euphemism in advertisements for Lifebuoy soap; box office, and also, the amount taken in at the b.o.; branch office

B/o brought over

b.o. back order; bad order; buyer's option

B.O.A. British Optical Association

B.O.A.C. British Overseas Airways Corporation

Boh., Bohem. Bohemia; Bohemian

Bol. Bolivia

bor. boron

bor. borough

bos'n boatswain

bot. botanical; botanist; botany; bottle; bottom; bought

Boul., boul. boulevard

B.P. Bachelor of Pharmacy; British Pharmacopoeia

B/P bills payable

Bp. Bishop

bp. birthplace

b/p blueprint

b.p. below proof; bill of parcels; boiling point

b.pd. bpd barrels per day

B. Pd., B. Pe. Bachelor of Pedagogy

B.P.E. Bachelor of Physical Education

B. Phil. Bachelor of Philosophy

BPI Bureau of Public Inquiries

bpl. birthplace

B.P.O.E. Benevolent and Protective Order of Elks

Bp. Suff. Bishop Suffragan

B.P.W.C. Business and Professional Women's Club

bq., bque. barque

Br bromine (Chem.)

B/R bills receivable

Br. British

br. branch; brand; brief; brig; bronze; brother

b.r. bills receivable; builder's risk

Braz. Brazil; Brazilian

B.R.C.S. British Red Cross Society

brd. board

b. rend. bill rendered

brev. brevet; brevetted; brevier (Typ.)

Br. Gu. British Guiana

Br. Hond. British Honduras

Brig Brigadier (US Army)

Brig. Gen. Brigadier General (GPO)

Brit. Britain; Britannia; Britannica; British

Bro., bro. brother

Br.Som. British Somaliland

B.R.T. Brotherhood of Railroad Trainmen

B.S. Bachelor of Science; Bachelor of Surgery; balance sheet; bull session (slang); abbreviation for a taboo expression for absurd, untrue talk

B/S bill of sale; bill of store

B/s, b/s bags, bales

b.s. balance sheet; bill of sale

B & S Brown and Sharpe gauge

B.S.A., BSA Boy Scouts of America

B.Sc. Bachelor of Science

B.S.Ed. Bachelor of Science in Education

B7d, b10d, b15d buyer 7(10,15) days to take up stock

bsk. basket

BT Boilerman (USN)

B.T., B.Th. Bachelor of Theology

Bt. Baronet

bt. boat; bought

b.t. berth terms (Shipping)

btk. buttock

btl. bottle

BTO Big Time Operator, in WWII military slang, a successful braggart; branch transportation Office (r)

btry battery (Mil.)

B.t.u. British thermal unit (usage of A.I.C.E.) Also B.T.U., B.Th.U., b.t.u., Btu, btu, and B

Bu butyl

BU Builder (USN)

B.U. Baptist Union; Boston University

Bu. Bureau

bu. bureau; bushel(s)

buck. buckram

Bucks Buckinghamshire (English county)

bul., bull. bulletin

Bulg. Bulgaria; Bulgarian

Bur. Bureau; Burma

B.S.U. Baptist Student Union

burl. burlesque

bus. business

b.v. book value

bvt. brevet; brevetted

B.W.I. British West Indies

bx. box

Byz. Byzantine; Bysantium

Bz. benzene

C

C carbon (Chem.); century: slang for hundred dollars, as in c-note; *centum* (L.) hundred

C — case; coupon; currency

C. Catholic; Celsius; Celtic; Centigrade; Centimeter; Chancellor; Chief; Church; City; Congress; Conservative; Consul; Corps

c. candle; capacity (Elec.); carat; carton; case; cathode; cent; center; centime; chapter; *circa* (L.) about; cubic; current

Ca calcium (Chem.)

CA chronological age

C.A. Catholic Action; Central America; Chartered Accountant; Chief Accountant; Commercial Agent; Consular Agent; Controller of Accounts

C/A capital account; credit account; current account

ca. cathode; centiare; *circa* (L.) about

CAA Civil Aeronautics Administration or Authority; Council of African Affairs

CAB Civil Aeronautics Board; Consumers' Advisory Board; Cooperative Analysis of Broadcasting

Caern. Caernarvonshire (Wales)

Caith. Caithness (Scotland)

Cal. California; large calorie

cal. calendar; caliber; calorie(s)

Calif. California (preferred)

Cam. Cameroons

Camb. Cambridge

Cambs. Cambridgeshire (England)

Camp. Campeche (Mexico)

Can. Canada; Canadian; Canon

can. canon; canto

canc. cancel; canceled; cancellation

c. and s.c. caps and small caps

Can. F. Canadian French

Can. Is. Canary Islands

Cant. Canterbury; Canticles; Cantonese

Cantab. *Cantabrigiensis* (L.) of Cambridge

Cantuar. *Cantuariensis* (L.) of Canterbury

CAP Civil Air Patrol

cap. capacity; capital; capitalize; capitulum; *caput* (L.) chapter

caps. capital letters; capsule

Capt. Captain

car. carat(s) (preferred)

Car. Carlow (Ireland)

Card. Cardiganshire (Wales); Cardinal

CARE Co-operative for American Remittances to Europe

Carib. Caribbean

Carm. Carmarthenshire (Wales)

carp. carpenter; carpentry

cat. catalogue; catechism

Cath. Cathedral; Catherine; Catholic

cav. cavalier; cavalry

CAVU, C.A.V.U.; c.a.v.u. ceiling and visibility unlimited (Aviation)

Cb columbium (Chem.)

CB cast brass

C.B. Cape Breton; cash book; currency bond; *Chirurgiae Baccalaureus* (L.) Bachelor of Surgery; Companion of the Bath

c.B. *col Básso* (Music)

CBC Canadian Broadcasting Corporation

C.B.D. cash before delivery

C.B.E. Commander of the British Empire

C.B.E.L. Cambridge Bibliography of English Literature

CBI China, Burma, India, a theatre of operations in WWII

C.B.I. Cape Breton Islands

CBS Columbia Broadcasting System

C.B.S. Confraternity of the Blessed Sacrament

CC cast copper

Cc cirro-cumulus (Meteor.)

C.C. cash credit; cashier's check; Catholic clergyman; Chief Clerk; City Council; City Councilor; County Clerk

cc. chapters; cubic centimeters

c.c. carbon copy; center to center; compass course; continuation clause

C. of C. Chamber of Commerce

CCA Commission for Conventional Armaments

C.C.A. Circuit Court of Appeals

CCC Civilian Conservation Corps; Commodity Credit Corporation

C.C.C. Christ's College, Cambridge; Corpus Christi College (Oxford)

C.C.F. Congregation of the Brothers of Charity; Cooperative Commonwealth Federation (of Canada)

C.Cls. Court of Claims

C.C.P. Code of Civil Procedure (legal); Court of Common Pleas

CCR Commission on Civil Rights

CCS Combined Chiefs of Staff

Cd cadmium (Chem.)

CD Driver (USN)

CD, C.D. Civil Defense

C.D. Colonial Dames

C/D certificate of deposit

cd. canned; cord; could

c.d. cash discount; cum dividend

cd. ft. cord foot (feet)

CDR, Cdr. Commander

Ce cerium (Chem.)

CE commutator end; Construction Electrician's Mate (USN)

C.E. Chemical Engineer; Chief Engineer; Christian Endeavor; Church of England; Civil Engineer; Corps of Engineers

c.e. *caveat emptor* (L.) buyer's risk; compass error

CEA Council of Economic Advisors

CED Committee for Economic Development

Cel. Celebes

cel. celebrated

Cels. Celsius (Temperature)

Celt. Celtic

cem. cement

cemb. *cembelo* (Music)

cemf counter electromotive force

cen. central; century

Cen. Amer. Central America

cent. centered; centigrade; centimeter; central; *centum* (L.) one hundred; century

ceram. ceramics

cert. certificate; certify; certiori

certif. certificate; certificated; certified; certify

cet. par. *ceteris paribus* (L.) other things being equal

Cey(l). Ceylon

Cf californium (Chem.)

C/f carried forward (accounting)

cf. calf (binding); *confer* (L.) compare

c.f. center fielder (Baseball)

c. & f. cost and freight

c.f.i., C.F.I. cost, freight, and insurance

c.f.m., cfm cubic feet per minute

C.G. Coast Guard; Commanding General; Consul General

c.g. center of gravity

cg., cg centigram(s)

C.G.S., c.g.s., cgs centimeter-gram-second (system)

CGT *Compagnie Generale Transatlantique* (The French Line); *Confederation Generale du Travail* (F.) General Confederation of Labor

CH casehardened

C.H. clearinghouse; Companion of Honor

Ch. Chaplain; Chapter; Chief; China; Chinese; choir (Music); Church

ch. chain; champion; chapter; check; chervonets (Russ. mon. unit); chervontsi (pl. of chervonets); child; choice

c.h. candle hours; courthouse; custom-house

Chald. Chaldaic; Chaldee

Chanc. Chancellor; Chancery

chap. chaplain; chapter

Chas. Charles

chauf. chauffeur

Ch. D. Doctor of Chemistry

Ch. E., Chem. E. Chemical Engineer

chem. chemical; chemist; chemistry

Ches(h). Cheshire (England)

chg. change; charge

chgd. changed; charged

Chi. Chicago

Chia. Chiapas (Mexico)

Chin. China; Chinese

Chino-Jap. Chino-Japanese

Chl. Chile

chm. chairman; checkmate

Ch. Org. choir organ (Music)

Chor. Chorus

Chr. Christ; Christian; Christopher

Chron. Chronicles

chron., chronol. chronological; chronology

chs. chapters

chtr. charter

Ci cirrus (Meteor.)

CI cast iron

C.I. Channel Islands; consular invoice

CIA Central Intelligence Agency

CIAA Coordinator of Inter-American Affairs

CIC Counterintelligence Corps (US Army)

C.I.D. Criminal Investigation Department (Brit.)

Cie *Compagnie* (F.) Company

C.I.F., c.i.f., cif cost, insurance and freight

CINC, C. in C., C in C, Cinc Commander in Chief (Mil.)

CINCAF, CINCLANT, CINPAC Commander in Chief, Asiatic (Fleet); Pacific (Fleet) (all USN)

CIO Congress of (formerly Committee for) Industrial Organizations

cir., circ. circa; circuit; circular; circulation; circumference

C.I.T. California Institute of Technology (better known abbreviated as Cal. Tech.)

cit. citation; cited; citizen; citrate

civ. civil; civilian; civilization; civilized

C.J. Chief Justice

ck. cask; check; cook

ckw. clockwise

Cl chlorine (Chem.)

CL center line

C.L. Canadian Legion; carload lots

Cl. Claude

cl. centiliter(s); claim; class; clause; clearance; clergyman; clerk; cloth

c.l. carload; carload lots

c.l. *col legno* (Music)

Cla. Clackmannan (Scotland)

Clar. Clarence; Clarendon (Typ.)

class. classic; classical; classification

C.L.D. Doctor of Civil Law

cld. called (bonds); cleared; colored

clin. clinical

clk. clerk; clock

C.L.U. Chartered Life Underwriter

Cm curium (Chem.)

C.M. Certified Master, or Mistress; *Chirugiae Magister* (L.) Master in Surgery; Congregation of the Mission (Vincentians, or Lazarists)

C/m call of more (stocks)

c.m., cm centimeter

c.m. church missionary; circular mil (wire measure); corresponding member; court-martial

cmdg. commanding

Cmdr. Commander

Cmdt. Commandant

C.M.G. Companion of (the Order of) St. Michael and St. George

cml. commercial

C.M.Mh. Missionaries of Marianhill

CMTC, C.M.T.C. Citizens' Military Training Camp

Cn cumulo-nimbus (Meteor.)

CN compass north

CNO Chief of Naval Operations (Mil.)

C.N.S., CNS central nervous system (Med.)

CO commanding officer (Mil.)

Co cobalt (Chem.)

C.O., CO conscientious objector

Co. company

Co., co. county

c.o., c/o care of; carried over

Coa. Coahuila (Mexico)

coad. coadjutor

c.o.d. cash on delivery

C. of S. Chief of Staff

cog, cognate

Col. Colombia; colonel; Colorado; Colossians; Columbia

col. collected; collector; college; colonel; colonial; colony; color; colored; column

Colim. Colima (Mexico)

coll. colleague; collect; collection; collective; collector; college; collegiate; colloquial

collab. collaborated; collaboration; collaborator

collat. collateral

colloq. colloquial; colloquialism; colloquially

Colm. column (Military)

Colo. Colorado

com. comedy; comma; commerce; commercial; commission; commissioner; committee; common; commonly; communication; community

Com. Commander; Commodore

Com. Err. The Comedy of Errors (Shak.)

COMINCH Commander-in-Chief (USN)

Cominform Communist Information Bureau, formed in 1947 to direct propaganda work of the Russian satellites

Comintern Communist International, founded in 1919 in Moscow, officially disbanded in 1943

coml. commercial

comm. commander; commerce; commissary; commission; committee; commonwealth

COMO, Como. Commodore

comp. comparative; comparison; compilation; compiled; composition; compositor; compound; comprising

compar. comparative

Comp. Dec. Comptroller's Decisions (US Treasury)

Comp. Gen. Comptroller General Decisions (US Treasury)

Compl. A Lover's Complaint (Shak.)

Comr. Commissioner

con. conclusion; *conjunx* (L.) wife (Law); connection; consolidated; consul; *contra* (L.) against; continued

conc. concentrate; concentrated; concentration; concerning

conch. conchology

cond. conducted (Mus.)

cond. conductivity; conductor

Con Ed Consolidated Edison Co. of N.Y.

conelrad control of electromagnetic radiation (Civil Defense)

con esp. *con espressione* (Music)

Conf. Confucian; Confucious

conf. *confer* (L.) compare; conference; confessor

Confed. Confederate

Cong. Congregational; Congress; Congressional

cong. *congius* (L.) gallon

Conglist. Congregationalist

Congr. Orat. Congregation of the Fathers of the Oratory of St. Philip Neri (Oration Fathers)

conj. conjugation; conjunction; conjunctive

Conn. Connecticut

cons. consecrated; consolidated; consonant; constable; constitution; constitutional; construction; consul; consulting

consol. consolidated

Consols consolidated annuities (part of British national debt)

Const. const. constable; constitution

constr. construction

Cont. Continental

cont. containing; contents; continent; continue; continued

contd. continued

contemp. contemporary

contr. contract; contraction; contralto; contrary

contrib. contribution; contributor

co-op. co-operative

Cop., Copt. Coptic

cop. copper; copyrighted

Cor. Corinthians (Biblical); Corsica

cor. corner; cornet; coroner; corrected; correction; correspondence; correspondent; corresponding

CORE Congress of Racial Equality

Coriol. Coriolanus (Shak.)

Corn., Cornw. Cornwall (England)

corol., coroll. corollary

Corp. Corporal; Corporation

corp., corpn. corporation

corr. correspond; correspondence; correspondent; corresponding

corresp. correspondence

C.O.S., c.o.s. cash on shipment

cos cosine

cos. companies; counties

cosec cosecant

cot cotangent

cp candlepower

cp. compare

c.p. chemically pure

CP command post; Communist Party; Construction Apprentice (USN)

C.P. Chief Patriarch; Common Prayer

CPA certified public accountant

cpd. compound

CPI Consumer Price Index

Cpl corporal (Mil.)

c.p.m. cycles per minute

CPO, C.P.O. Chief Petty Officer (USN)

CQ Charge of Quarters (Mil.)

C.R. Congregation of the Resurrection (Resurrectionist Fathers); Costa Rica

Cr chromium (Chem.)

Cr. Cranch (US Supreme Court Reports)

cr. credit; creditor; creek

craniol. craniology

C-ration Emergency ration WW II

C.R.C. Coordinating Research Council

cres., cresc. crescendo

crim. con. criminal conversation

crit. critical; criticism

CRP C-reactive protein

cryst. crystallized; crystalline; crystallography

Cs cesium (Chem.); cirro-stratus (Meteor.)

C.S. Christian Science; Christian Scientist

C.S., c.s. capital stock; civil service

C/S, cs. cases

C.S.A. Confederate States of America

CSC Civil Service Commission

C.S.C. Conspicuous Service Cross

csc cosecant

C.S.D. Doctor of Christian Science

csk. cask

CSigO, C.S.O. Chief Signal Officer

C.S.P. Congregation of St. Paul the Apostle (Paulist Fathers)

CSS Commodity Stabilization Service

c.s.t. central standard time

Ct. Connecticut

ct. cent(s); county; court

ctn. cotangent

ctr. center

cts. centimes; cents

Cu cumulus (Meteorol.); *cuprum* (L.) copper (Chem.)

cu. cubic

cu. cm. cubic centimeter

cu. ft. cubic foot

cu. in. or **in³** cubic inch

Cumb. Cumberland (England)

Cur. Curacao

cur. currency; current

C.V.Is. Cape Verde Islands

cv., cvt. convertible (bonds)

C.V.O. Commander of the (Royal) Victorian Order

CW continuous wave

CWA Civil Works Administration

CWO chief warrant officer (Mil.)

C.W.O., c.w.o cash with order

CWS Chemical Warfare Service

cwt. hundredweight

cyc. cyclopedia; cyclopedic

cyclo. cyclotron

cyl. cylinder; cylindrical

Cymb. Cymbeline (Shak.)

C.Y.O. Catholic Youth Organization

Cyp. Cyprian; Cypriote; Cyprus

C.Z. Canal Zone

Czech. Czechoslovakia

D

D deuterium (Chem.); Department (US Army); 500

D. December; *Deus* (L.) God; Doctor; *Dominus* (L.) Lord; Don; Duchess; Duke; Dutch

D., d. *da* (L.) give (Pharm.); dam (in pedigrees); date; daughter; day, or days; dead; *decretum* (L.) degree; democrat; democratic; denarii; denarius; density (Physics); deputy; diameter; died; dinar; dollar; door (Theat.); dose; dowager; drachma

d. dyne; pence

d. dextro (Chem.)

DA Department of the Army

D.A. District Attorney

da. daughter; day; days

D.A.B., DAB Dictionary of American Biography

D.Agr. Doctor of Agriculture

dal., dal decaliter

Dall. Dallas' US Supreme Court Reports

Dan., Danl. Daniel

Dan. Danish

D.A.R. Daughters of the American Revolution

D.Arch. Doctor of Architecture

dat. dative

DATA Defense Air Transportation Administration

dau. daughter

DAV, D.A.V. Disabled American Veterans

db decibel

d.b.a. doing business as

D.B.E. Dame Commander of the British Empire

d.b.h. diameter at breast height (Forestry)

D. Bib. Douay Bible

dbl. double

DC Damage Controlman (USN)

D.C. *da capo* (Music); District of Columbia; Doctor of Chiropractic

DC, D.C., d.c. direct current

D.C.L. Doctor of Canon Law; Doctor of Civil Law

D.C.M. Distinguished Conduct Medal (British Army)

DD daily double

D.D. *Divinitatus Doctor* (L.) Doctor of Divinity

D.D., D/D demand draft

dd., d/d delivered

D/D, D/d, d.d. days after date, or days' (day's) date

D-day In military planning, the day of operation (D-day WW I was the St. Mihiel offensive; WW II, the Normandy invasion, June 6, 1944)

D.D.S. Doctor of Dental Surgery

D.D.Sc. Doctor of Dental Science

DDT dichlorodiphenyltrichloroethane (GPO)

DE Destroyer Escort

D.E. Doctor of Engineering; Doctor of Entomology

Dea. Deacon

deb., deben., debenture

Dec. December

dec. deceased; declaration; declension; declination; decrease

dec., decim. decimeter

decd. deceased

decl. declension

def. defendant; deferred; defined; definite; definition

deg. degree; degrees

D.E.I. Dutch East Indies

Del. Delaware

del. delegate

Dem. Democrat; Democratic

Den. Denmark

Denb., Denbh. Denbighshire (Wales)

D.Eng. Doctor of Engineering

denom. denomination

dent. dentist; dentistry

Dep., dep. deposit

dep. department; departs; departure; deponent; depot; deputy

dept. department; deputy

der., deriv. derivation; derivative; derive; derived

Derby Derbyshire (England)

Derry Londonderry (Ireland)

desc. descendant

D. ès L. *Docteur ès Lettres* (F.) Doctor of Letters

D. ès S. *Docteur ès Sciences* (F.) Doctor of Sciences

det. detachment (Mil.)

Deut. Deuteronomy (Biblical)

Dev., Devon Devonshire (England)

DEW distant early warning (DEWline)

DF, D/F, D.F. direction finding

D.F. *Defensor Fidei* (L.) Defender of the Faith; Federal District (Mexico)

D.F.C. Distinguished Flying Cross (US & Brit.)

dg. decigram

D.H.L. Doctor of Hebrew Literature

DI drill instructor; drill sergeant

Di didymium (Chem.)

di., dia., diam. diameter

dial. dialectic; dialectal

diap. diapason (Music)

dict. dictator; dictionary

diff. difference; different

dig. digest

dim., dimin. diminutive

dim., dimin. diminuendo (Music)

din. dinar

dipl. diplomatic

dir. director

disc. discount; discovered

disch. discharged

dist. distance; distinguish; distinguished; district

Dist. Atty. District Attorney

Dist. Ct. District Court

distr. distribute; distribution; distributor

div division (US Army)

div. divided; dividend; division; divisor; divorced

D.J. disc jockey; District Judge; *Doctor Juris* (L.) Doctor of Law

D.J.S. Doctor of Juridical Science

dkg. dekagram

dkl. dekaliter

dkm. dekameter

D/L Demand Loan

dl deciliter

DLF Development Loan Fund

D. Lit(t)., Lit(t). D. *Doctor Lit(t)-erarum* (L.) Doctor of Literature, or of Letters

D.L.S. Doctor of Library Science

DM, Dm Deutsche mark

D.M. Deputy Master; Doctor of Mathematics; Doctor of Medicine; Doctor of Music

dm. decimeter

DMB Defense Mobilization Board

D.M.D. *Dentariae Medicinae Doctor* (L.) Doctor of Dental Medicine

DMEA Defense Minerals Exploration Administration

D.M.S. Director of Medical Services; Doctor of Medical Sciences

D.Mus. Doctor of Music

D.N.B. Dictionary of National Biography (British)

DO Defense Order (Mil.)

D.O. Doctor of Optometry; Doctor of Ostepathy

do. *ditto* (It.) the same

DOA D.O.A. dead on arrival

doc. document

dol. $; dollar

dom. domestic; dominion

Dom. Rep. Dominican Republic

Don. Donegal (Ireland)

Dorset Dorsetshire (England)

doz. dozen

DP displaced person (US Govt.)

DP, D.P. degree of polymerization; diametrical pitch

D.P.H. Diploma in Public Health; Doctor of Public Health

D.Phil. Doctor of Philosophy

dpt. department; deponent

D.R. Dutch Reformed

D.R., D/R, d.r. dead reckoning; deposit receipt

Dr. doctor; drive

dr. debit; debtor; drachma; dram; drams; drawer

dram. pers. dramatis personae

D-ration See C- and K- rations

D.S. *Dal Segno* (Music)

d.s. days after sight (Com.)

D.S., D. Sc. Doctor of Science

D.S.C., DSC Distinguished Service Cross

D.S.M., DSM Distinguished Service Medal

D.S.O. (Companion of the) Distinguished Service Order; District Staff Officer

D.S.T. Doctor of Sacred Theology

d.s.t. daylight saving time

d.t. delirium tremens

D. Th., D. Theol. Doctor of Theology

Du. Duke; Dutch

Dub. Dublin (Ireland, city & county)

Dumb. Dumbarton (Scotland)

Dumf. Dumfries (county in Scotland)

dup. duplicate

Dur. Durango (Mexico); Durham (England)

DV distinguished visitor (Air Force)

D.V. *Deo volente* (L.) God willing; by God's will; Douay Version

D.V.M. Doctor of Veterinary Medicine

D/W dock warrant

d.w.t. deadweight tons

dwt. denarius weight, i.e., pennyweight

DX, D.X. distance (Radio)

Dy dysprosium (Chem.)

dyn., dynam. dynamics

dz. dozen

E

E. Earl; Earth; east; eastern; English

e. engineer; engineering; entrance; erg

E.A., EA educational age (Psychol.)

ea. each

e. & o.e. errors and omissions excepted

Eb erbium (Chem.)

ECA Economic Cooperation Administration

eccl., eccles. ecclesiastic

Eccles., Eccl. Ecclesiastes (Biblical)

Ecclus. Ecclesiasticus (Biblical)

ecol. ecological; ecology

econ. economic; economics; economy

E.C.U. English Church Union

Ecua. Ecuador

ed. edited; edition; editor

Ed.B., Ed.D., Ed.M., Bachelor of Education; Doctor of Education; Master of Education

edit. edited; edition

e.d.t. eastern daylight time

educ. education; educational

Edw. Edward

E.E. electrical engineer

EEE eastern equine encephalitis

EEG electroencephalogram

Eg. Egypt; Egyptian

e.g. *exemple gratia* (L.) for example

Egyptol. Egyptology

EHF extremely high frequency

E.I. East Indian; East Indies

EKG electrocardiogram

E.L. East Lothian (Scotland)

elec., elect. electric; electrical; electrician; electricity

elem. elementary; element(s)

elev. elevation

Eliz. Elizabeth; Elizabethan

E. long. east longitude

EM enlisted men (Mil.)

Em. emanation (Chem.); Emily; Emma

embryol. embryology

e.m.f. electromotive force

Emp. Emperor; Empress

e.m.u. electromagnetic unit(s)

enc., encl. enclosure

ency., encyc., encycl. encyclopedia

Ency. Brit., Encyc. Brit. Encyclopedia Brittanica

ENE east-northeast

Eng. England; English

eng. engine; engineer; engineering; engraved; engraver; engraving

Eng. D. Doctor of Engineering

engin. engineering

engr. engineer; engraved; engraver; engraving

Ens. ensign

entom. entomology

env. envelope

e.o.m. end of month

Eph., Ephes. Ephesians

Epiph. Epiphany

Epis., Episc. Episcopalian

EQ educational quotient

eq. equal; equalizer; equalizing; equation; equivalent

equiv. equivalent

Er erbium (Chem.)

ERA Emergency Relief Administration

ERP European Recovery Program

E.R.V. English Revised Version (of the Bible)

erron. erroneous

ESC Economic and Social Council

ESE east-southeast

Esd. Esdras (Biblical)

Esk. Eskimo

ESP extrasensory perception

esp., espec. especially

espress. espressivo (Music)

Esq., Esqr. Esquire

Ess. Essex (England)

e.s.t. eastern standard time

Est. Estonia

est. established

Esth. Esther

e.s.u. electrostatic unit(s)

ET electronics technician (USN)

e.t. eastern time

ETA estimated time of arrival

et al. et alii (L.) and others

etc. *et cetera* (L.) and so forth

Eth. Ethiopia

ethnol. ethnology

ETO European Theater of Operations (Mil.)

et seq. *et sequens* (L.) and the following; *et sequentes* or *sequentia* (L.) and those that follow

etym., etymol. etymological; etymology

E.U. Evangelical Union

Eu europium (Chem.)

Eur. Europe; European

Euratom European Atomic Energy Community

E.V. English Version (of the Bible)

Ex. Doc. executive document

Exod. Exodus (Biblical)

Ez., Ezr. Ezra (Biblical)

Ezek. Ezekial (Biblical)

F

F Fahrenheit; farad; fathom; fluorine (Chem.); function (Math.)

F. Fahrenheit; February; Fellow; France; French

f forte (Music)

f. farad; farthing; fathom; feminine; fine; fluid (ounce); folio; following; franc; frequency

f., ff. and following page(s)

FA field artillery (US Army)

f.a. free alongside (Shipping)

FAA Federal Aviation Agency

F.A.A.S. Fellow of the American Association for the Advancement of Science; Fellow of the American Academy of Arts and Sciences

FAdm Fleet Admiral (USN)

Falk.Is. Falkland Islands

F.A.M., F. and A.M. Free and Accepted Masons

fam. familiar; family

FAO Food and Agriculture Organization

f.a.s. free alongside ship

FAS Foreign Agricultural Service

F.B.A. Fellow of the British Academy

FBI Federal Bureau of Investigation

f.c. follow copy (Print.)

FCA Farm Credit Administration

FCC Federal Communications Commission

F.C.C. First Class Certificate

FCIC Federal Crop Insurance Corporation

fcp. foolscap

F.C.S. Fellow of the Chemical Society

FDA Food and Drug Administration

FDIC Federal Deposit Insurance Corporation

F.D.R., FDR Since the dropping of periods in the abbreviations of governmental agencies became widespread during the reign of Franklin Delano Roosevelt it might be fitting that the short form by which he was most commonly nicknamed be designated without periods.

Fe ferrum (iron) (Chem.)

FEB Fair Employment Board

Feb. February

fec. fecit (L.) He (or she) made (or executed) it

Fed. Federal Reporter

fed. federal; federated; federation

fem. feminine

FEPC Fair Employment Practices Committee

Fer. Fermanagh (Ireland)

FERA Federal Emergency Relief Administration

ff fortissimo (Music) very loud

F.F.A., f.f.a. free from alongside

FFC Foreign Funds Control

fff fortississimo (Music) as loud as possible

F.F.V. First Families of Virginia

FHA Farmers Home Administration; Federal Housing Administration

FHLBB Federal Home Loan Bank Board

F.H.S. Fellow of the Heraldry Society; Fellow of the Horticultural Society

F.I. Falkland Islands

FICA Federal Insurance Contributions Act

fid. fiduciary

fig. figurative; figuratively; figure; figures

Fin. Finland; Finnish

fin. financial

f.i.o. free in and out (shipping)

fir. firkin

1st Lt. first lieutenant (GPO)

1st Sgt. first sergeant (GPO)

Fl fluorine (Chem.)

Fl. Flanders; Flemish

fl. florin; *floruit* (L.) he flourished; flourished

Fla. Florida

flak *fliegerabwehrkanone* (G) anti-aircraft artillery, and the explosions of anti-aircraft shells

fld. field

Flint. Flintshire (Wales)

F.L.N., FLN *Front de Liberation Nationale* (F.) Algerian nationalist organization

FM frequency modulation

fm. fathom; from

FMB Federal Maritime Board

FMCS Federal Mediation and Conciliation Service

fn. footnote

FNMA Federal National Mortgage Association (Fannie Mae)

F.O. Foreign Office

F.O., f.o. field officer

F.O.B., f.o.b. free on board

F.O.E. Fraternal Order of Eagles

fol. folio; following

foll. following

for. foreign; forestry

F.O.R., f.o.r. free on rail

fort. fortification; fortified

forz. forzando (Music) with force

4-H an agricultural program for youth to improve head, heart, hands and health

F.P., f.p. foot-pound; freezing point

fp forte, and then, *piano* (Music) the note is to be strongly accented

FPC Federal Power Commission

FPIS forward propagation ionospheric scatter

f.p.m. feet per minute

FPO fleet post office

f.p.s. feet per second; frames per second

FPV free piston vessel

F.R. Federal Register

Fr francium (Chem.)

Fr. Father; France; Francis; *Frater* (L.) brother; French; Friday

F.R.A. Fellow of the Royal Academy; thus F.R.C.S. is Fellow of the Royal College of Surgeons, etc.

Frdk. Frederick

freq. frequent; frequentative; frequently

Fr.Gu. French Guiana

Fri. Friday

Fris., Frs. Frisian

FRS Federal Reserve System

F.R.S. Fellow of the Royal Society

Fr.Som. French Somaliland

frt. freight

FS Forest Service

F.S.Arch. Fellow of the Society of Architects

F.S.C. Brothers of the Christian Schools (Christian Brothers)

F.S.C.J. Congregation of the Sons of the Sacred Heart of Jesus

FSH follicle-stimulating hormone

FSR, F.S.R. Field Service Regulations

F. Supp. Federal Supplement

ft. foot

ft. b.m. foot board measure

ft.-c. footcandle

FTC Federal Trade Commission

fthm. fathom

ft.-l. foot-lambert

ft.-lb. foot-pound

fubar fouled (euphemism) up beyond all recognition, WW II military slang

furn. furnished

furng. furnishing

fut. future

f.v. *folio verso* (L.) on the back of the page

f.w. fresh water

FWA Federal Works Agency

F.W.B. Freewill Baptist

fwd. forward

FYI for your information

fz. forzándo (Music), also *forz.*

F.Z.S. Fellow of the Zoological Society

G

G grand: slang for thousand dollars; God (in Masonic symbol)

G. German; specific gravity

G., g. conductance (Elec.); gauge; gourde; grain; guinea; gulf

g. gram

g general intelligence

G1, G2, G3, G4 Asst. Chief of Staff, G-1, Personnel; G-2, Intelligence; G-3, Operations; G-4, Logistics (US Army)

Ga gallium (Chem.)

Ga. Gallic; Georgia

GA, G.A. General Agent; General Assembly

G.A., g.a. general average

Gael. Gaelic

Gal. Galatians (Biblical); Galen; Galway (Ireland)

gal., gall. gallon; gallons

gals. gallons

glv. galvanic

GAO General Accounting Office

G.A.R. Grand Army of the Republic

GARIOA Government and Relief in Occupied Areas

GAW guaranteed annual wage

gaz. gazette; gazetteer

G.B. Great Britain

G.B.E. Knight (or Dame) Grand Cross of the British Empire

G.B.S. George Bernard Shaw

GCA ground control approach (Aviation)

G.C.B. Grand Cross of the Bath (Knight)

G.C.D., g.c.d. greatest common divisor

GCI ground controlled interception (station) (Mil.)

GCR ground controlled radar (Mil.)

GCT, G.C.T., G.c.t. (Preferred) Greenwich civil time

G.C.V.O. (Knight) Grand Cross of the (Royal) Victorian Order

G.D. Grand Duchess; Grand Duchy; Grand Duke

Gd gadolinium (Chem.)

g.d. God-damned. Here is a good example of the use of the abbreviation as a euphemism for the semi-taboo expression. Cf. **p.o.**, **t.s.**, etc.

gde. gourde (Haitian monetary unit)

gds. goods

Ge germanium (Chem.)

g.e. gilt edges (Bookbinding)

geb. *gebornen* (G.) born

Gen. General (Army); Genesis; Geneva; Genevan

gen. gender; genera; general; generally; genitive; genus

geneal. genealogy

genit. genitive

genl. general

gent. gentleman

Geo. George

geod. geodesy; geodetic

geog. geographer; geographic; geographical; geography

geol. geologic; geological; geologist; geology

geom. geometer; geometric; geometrical; geometry

Ger. German; Germany

ger. gerund

gest. *gestorben* (G.) died

Gestapo *Geheime Staatspolizei* (G.) Secret State Police (of Nazi Germany)

GG gamma globulin (Med.)

g.gr. great gross

GHA Greenwich hour angle (Navigation)

GHQ General Headquarters (Military)

GI general issue; Government issue; the nickname for an American foot soldier in WW II and afterward, for any returning serviceman, as "ex-GI"

gi. gill; gills

Gib. Gibraltar

Gk. Greek

Gl glucinium or glucinum (Chem.)

Glam., Glamorg. Glamorganshire (Wales)

gld. guilder (Dutch monetary unit)

Glos Gloucestershire (England)

gloss. glossary

GM Gunner's Mate (USN)

G.M. General Manager; George Medal (Brit.); Grand Master

gm. gram(s)

G-man Government man, specifically, an agent of the FBI

G.m.a.t. Greenwich mean astronomical time

G.M.B. Grand Master of the Bath

G.M. & S. general, medical, and surgical

GMT, G.M.T., G.m.t. (Preferred) Greenwich mean time

GO General Orders (US Army)

GOP, G.O.P. Grand Old Party (the Republican party)

Goth., goth. Gothic

Gov., gov. governor

Govt., govt. government

G.P. general paresis; general practitioner; *Gloria Patri* (L.) Glory to the Father

GPM, g.p.m. (Preferred), **gpm** gallons per minute

GPO, G.P.O. General Post Office; Government Printing Office

g.p.s. gallons per second

G.P.U. (R.) The Soviet secret police which succeeded the Cheka in 1922; called also **Ogpu**

GQ, G.Q., g.q. general quarters (Nav.)

Gr. Grecian; Greece; Greek

gr. grain; grains; gram; grams; gross

grad. graduate; graduated

gram. grammar; grammarian; grammatical

Gr. Br., Gr. Brit. Great Britain

Grc. Greece

Grnld. Greenland

gro. gross

Gr. Org. Great Organ (Music)

gr. wt. gross weight

GS, G.S. General Staff

GSA General Services Administration

G.S.A. Girl Scouts of America

gt. great

G.T.C., g.t.c. good till canceled, or countermanded

GTS gas turbine ship

Guan. Guanajuato (Mexico)

guar. guaranteed

Guat. Guatemala

Guer. Guerrero (Mexico)

gun. gunnery

gynecol. gynecological; gynecology

H

H henry (Elec.); heroin (Colloq.); hydrogen (H2 deutorum) (Chem.); intensity of magnetic field (Physics)

H., h. harbor; hard; hardness; height; high; hour; husband

h. henry (Elec.)

ha. hectare(s)

h.a. *hoc anno* (L.) in this year

Hab. Habakkuk (Biblical)

Hag. Haggai (Biblical)

Hai. Haiti

Hal. halogen (Chem.)

Ham. Hamlet, Prince of Denmark (Shak.)

Hants Hampshire (England)

Harv. Harvard

Hb hemoglobin

H.B.M. His (or Her) Britannic Majesty

H-bomb hydrogen bomb

H.C. Holy Communion; House of Commons

hcf, h.c.f. highest common factor

h.c.l. high cost of living (Colloq.)

H.C.M. His (or Her) Catholic Majesty

H. Con. Res. (with number) House concurrent resolution

hd. head

hdkf. handkerchief

H. Doc. (with number) House document

hdqrs. headquarters

HE high explosive (Mil.)

He helium (Chem.)

H.E. His Eminence; His Excellency

Heb. Hebrews (Biblical)

Hen. Henry

1 Hen. IV First Part of King Henry IV (Shak.)

2 Hen. IV Second Part of King Henry IV (Shak.)

Hen. V King Henry V (Shak.)

1 Hen. VI First Part of King Henry VI (Shak.)

2 Hen. VI Second Part of King Henry VI (Shak.)

3 Hen. VI Third Part of King Henry VI (Shak.)

Hen. VIII King Henry VIII (Shak.)

her. heraldry

Heref. Herefordshire (England)

Herts Hertsfordshire (England)

HEW Department of Health, Education and Welfare

HF (Preferred), **H.F., h.f.** high frequency

Hf hafnium (Chem.)

hf. half

hf. bd. half-bound (Bookbinding)

hf. cf. half-calf (Bookbinding)

hf. mor. half-morocco (Bookbinding)

Hg *hydrargyrum* (NL.) mercury (Chem.)

hg. hectogram; heliogram

H.H. His, or Her, Highness; His Holiness (the Pope)

hhd. hogshead

HHFA Housing and Home Finance Agency

H.I. Hawaiian Islands; not the state of Hawaii

Hid. Hidalgo (Mexico)

hi-fi high fidelity

H.I.H. His (Her) Imperial Highness

H.I.M. His (Her) Imperial Majesty

Hind. Hindu; Hindustan; Hindustani

hist. historian; historical; history

H.J. *hic jacet* (L.) here lies; — used in epitaphs

H.J. Res. (with number) House joint resolution

H.L. House of Lords

hl. hectoliter

HLBB Home Loan Bank Board

H.M. His (Her) Majesty

hm. hectometer

H.M.S. His (Her) Majesty's Service, Ship or Steamer

Ho holmium (Chem.)

ho. house

HOLC Home Owners' Loan Corporation

Hon. Honorable

hon. honorably; honorary

Hond. Honduras

Hong K. Hong Kong

Hor. Horace

hor. horizon; horizontal

horol. horology

hort. horticultural; — culture

Hos. Hosea (Biblical)

hosp. hospital

How. Howard (U.S. Supreme Court Reports)

how howitzer (Mil.)

H.P. High Priest

HP, H.P., hp, h.p., hp. high-powered; horsepower

HQ, H.Q., hq, h.q. headquarters (Mil.)

Hq Co Headquarters Company (Mil.)

H.R. Home Rule, or Ruler; House of Representatives; (with number) House Bill

hr. hour; hours

H. Rept. (with number) House report

H. Res. (with number) House resolution

H.R.H. His (Her) Royal Highness

hrs. hours

H.S.T., HST Harry Truman was never as widely known by his initials as was his predecessor. The most interesting thing about these initials, of course, is that the S stands for nothing.

Ht. Harriet

ht. heat; height

Hts. Heights

Hung. Hungarian; Hungary

Hunts Huntingdonshire (England)

Hy. Henry

hyd., hydros. hydrostatics

hyd., hydraul. hydraulics

hydraul. hydraulics

hyp., hypoth. hypothesis

hypo hyposulphite of soda (photography)

I

I iodine (Chem.)

I. Island(s); Isle(s)

i. intransitive; island

Ia. Iowa (Not Official) This as with many similar entries is included only for the record and not with our, or the post office's, approval.

IADB Inter-American Defense Board

IAEA International Atomic Energy Agency

IAS indicated air speed (Aviation)

IATSE International Alliance of Theatrical Stage Employees and Moving Picture Machine Operators of the United States and Canada

ib., ibid. *ibidem* (L.) in the same place

I.B.S.A. International Bible Students' Association (Jehovah's Witnesses)

ICA International Cooperation Administration

ICBM intercontinental ballistic missile (Mil.)

ICC Interstate Commerce Commission

Ice., Icel. Iceland; Icelandic

ichth. ichthyology

ICI, I.C.I. Imperial Chemical Industries (Brit.); International Committee on Illumination

ICJ International Court of Justice

I.C.S. Indian Civil Service

Id. Idaho (Not official)

id. *idem* (L.) the same

ID, I.D., i.d. inside diameter

I.D. identification, as "I.D. Card"; Intelligence Department; Iraqi dinar

IDP International Driving Permit

IE, I.E. Indo-European

i.e. *id est* (L.) that is

IF, I.F., i.f., i-f intermediate frequency

IFC International Finance Corporation

IFF identification, friend or foe (Mil. radar)

I.F.S. Irish Free State. Now historical.

IG Inspector General (Mil.)

I.G. Indo-Germanic

ign. ignition

I.G.Y. International Geophysical Year (July 1957-December 1958)

IHP, I.H.P., ihp, i.h.p., i. hp. indicated horsepower

IHS, I.H.S. A symbol or monogram representing the Greek contraction for Jesus

Il ilinium (Chem.)

Ill. Illinois

ill., illus., illust. illustrated; illustration

ILO International Labor Organization

I.L.P. Independent Labour Party (Brit.)

ILS instrument landing system (Aviation)

I.M. Isle of Man (Britain)

IMCCO Intergovernmental Maritime Consultative Organization

imit. imitation; imitative

immunol. immunology

Imp. Imperator

imp. imperative; imperfect; imperial; impersonal; import; imported; importer; *imprimatur* (L.) let it be printed

imper. imperative

imperf. imperfect; imperforated

imp. gal. imperial gallon

impv. imperative

In indium (Chem.)

in. inch

inc. inclosure; including; inclusive; income; incorporated; increase

inch., incho. inchoative (grammar)

incl. inclosure; inclusive

incog. incognito

incor., incorp. incorporated

incr. increased; increasing

Ind. India; Indian; Indiana; Indies

ind. independent; index; indicative; indigo; industrial

indecl. indeclinable

indef. indefinite

indic. indicating; indicative

indiv. individual

induc. induction

inf. infinitive; information

INF, inf, Inf. infantry

infin. infinitive

init. initial

in.-lb. inch pound

in loc. cit. *in loco citato* (L.) in the place cited

inorg. inorganic

I.N.R.I. *Iesus (Jesus) Nazarenus, Rex Iudaeorum (Judaeorum)* (L.) Jesus of Nazareth, King of the Jews

INS International News Service (Since 1959, combined with UP, to form UPI)

ins. inches; inspector; insular; insulated; insulator; insurance

insep. inseparable

insp. inspector

Insp. Gen. Inspector General (Mil.)

Inst. Institute; Institution

inst. instant (the present month); instrumental

instr. instructor; instrument; instruments; instrumental

int. intelligence; interest; interior; interjection; internal; international; intransitive

interj. interject

internat. international

interrog. interrogative

intr., intrans. intransitive

Int. Rev. Internal Revenue

introd. introduction; introductory

Inv. Inverness (Scotland)

inv. inventor; invoice

invt. inventory

Io ionium (Chem.)

I.O.F. Independent Order of Foresters

I.O.O.F. Independent Order of Odd Fellows

I.O.R.M. Improved Order of Red Men

I O U, IOU, I.O.U. I owe you

I.O.W. Isle of Wight (Britain)

IPA International Phonetic Association or Alphabet

IQ, I.Q. intelligence quotient

i.q. *idem quod* (L.) the same as

Ir iridium (Chem.)

Ir. Ireland; Irish

I.R.A. Irish Republican Army (now outlawed)

Iran. Iranian

IRBM intermediate range ballistic missile (Mil.)

IRE Institute of Radio Engineers

Ire. Ireland

IRO International Refugee Organization

irreg. irregular; irregularly

IRS Internal Revenue Service

Is. Isaiah (Biblical) This too is simply for the record, not with approval.

Is., is. island; islands; isle

Isa. Isaiah (Biblical)

Isl(s)., isl(s). islands

Isr. Israel

It., Ital. Italian; Italy

ital. italic (type)

ITO International Trade Organization

ITU International Telecommunication Union; International Typographical Union

IU, I.U. international unit(s) (Biol., Immunol., etc.) (Measuring amount and effect of a vitamin.)

I.U.T.A.M. International Union of Theoretical and Applied Mechanics

I.W. Isle of Wight (Britain)

IWW, I.W.W. Industrial Workers of the World, a labor organization which once wielded great influence in the USA, and whose members were termed "Wobblies"

J

J joule (but GPO prefers j.) (Physics)

J. Job (Biblical); Joel (Biblical); Judge; Justice

Ja, Ja. January

JA, J.A. Judge Advocate (Mil.)

Jal. Jalisco (Mexico)

Jam. Jamaica

Jan, Jan. January

Jap. Japan; Japanese

Jas. James (Biblical)

jato jet-assisted takeoff

Jav. Javanese

J.C. Jesus Christ

J.C.D. *Juris Canonici Doctor* (L.) Doctor of Canon Law; *Juris Civilis Doctor* (L.) Doctor of Civil Law

jct., jctn. junction

J.D. *Jurum Doctor* (L.) Doctor of Laws; juvenile delinquency

J.D.C. American Jewish Joint Distribution Committee; also known as "the Joint"

Je, Je. June This is, of course, ridiculous, but it is so listed by the most powerful authority in U.S. lexicography, which also lists **Jy** for July and **My** for May. We suggest all three be dropped and hope that future lexicographers will have similar courage.

Jer. Jeremiah (Biblical); Jeremy

JFK John Fitzgerald Kennedy

jg, j.g. junior grade

JHVH (also **IHVHVH** and **YHVH**) the Hebrew incommunicable name of the Supreme Being

Jl. July. See comments under **Je** and elsewhere

Jno. John

JO journalist (USN)

Jo. Josephine

Jo. Bapt. John the Baptist

Jo. Div. John the Divine

Jo. Evang. John the Evangelist

Jon., Jona. Jonah (Biblical); Jonathan

Jos. Joseph; Josiah

Josh. Joshua (Biblical)

jour. journal; journeyman

J.P. justice of the peace

Jr., jr. junior

J.S.D. Doctor of Juridical Science

Judg. Judges (Biblical)

Judge Adv. Gen. Judge Advocate General

Jul. Jules; Julius; July

Jul. Caes. Julius Caesar (Shak.)

Jun., jun. junior

Junc., junc. junction

Jur. D. *Juris Doctor* (L.) Doctor of Law

jurisp. jurisprudence

jus., just. justice

J.W. Jehovah's Witnesses. See **I.B.S.A.**

J.W.V. Jewish War Veterans

K

K cumulus (Meteorol.); *kalium* (L.) potassium; king (Chess); kruna (Czech. mon. unit)

K. Kelvin (Temperature)

K., k. *kalendae* (L.) calends; kilogram; king; knight; kopeck; krone

k kilo-(thousand)

k. capacity (Elec.); carat (Assaying); constant

ka. kathode or cathode

kal. kalends

Kans., Kan., Kas. Kansas (**Kans.** preferred)

Kath. Katherine

KB king's bishop (Chess)

K.B. King's Bench; Knight Bachelor; Knight of the Bath

K.C. King's Counsel

K.C., K. of C. Knights of Columbus

kc, kc. kilocycle(s)

Kc korun; koruna; koruny (Czech.)

kcal. kilocalorie

K.C.B. Knight Commander of the Bath

K.C.V.O. Knight Commander of the (Royal) Victorian Order

K.D. knocked down (Com.)

Kev. kilo electron volts

K.G. Knight (of the Order) of the Garter

kg, kg. keg(s)

kg. kilogram

kil. kilometer(s)

kilo. kilogram; kilometer

kilog. kilogram

kilol. kiloliter

kilom. kilometer

Kild. Kildare (Ireland)

Kilk. Kilkenny (Ireland)

Kin. Kinross (Scotland)

Kinc. Kincardine (Scotland)

Kirk. Kirkcudbright (Scotland)

K. John King John (Shak.)

K.K.K. Ku Klux Klan; not Klu

K Kt king's knight (Chess)

kl., kl kiloliter

km., km kilometer; kingdom

knt. knight

KO, K.O., k.o. knockout (Pugilism)

K. of C. Knight, or Knights, of Columbus

K. of P. Knight, or Knights, of Pythias

kop. kopeck(s) (U.S.S.R.)

KP king's pawn (Chess)

K.P. Knight (of the Order) of St. Patrick; Knights of Pythias

K.P., KP kitchen police (Mil.)

KR king's rook (Chess)

Kr krypton (Chem.)

kr kreutzer; krone

K-ration See C- and D- rations

Krs kurus (Turkey)

Kt knight

kt. carat; kiloton

kv. kilovolt

kv.-a. kilovolt-ampere

kw. kilowatt

kw.-hr. (preferred), K.W.H., kwh, kw-hr kilowatt-hour

K.T. Knight Templar; Knight (of the Order) of the Thistle (Scotland)

Kuw. Kuwait

Ky. Kentucky

L

£, L, l. *libra* (L.) pound

L left (hand) (Music); length (Physics); longitude (Geod.)

L, l coefficient of inductance (Elec.)

L. Latin; Licentiate; Linnaeus (Botany); Lodge (Fraternal)

L., l. lake; land; latitude; law; leaf; league; left; lempira (Honduras); length; leu; lev; lex; *liber* (L.) book; line; link; lira, lire (t.); low

l. liter

l-, l. levo-. (Chem.)

La lanthanum (Chem.)

La. Louisiana

L.A. Latin America; Library Association; Local Agent; Los Angeles

Lab. Labrador

lab. laboratory

Lam. Lamentations (Biblical)

Lancs Lancashire (England)

lang. language

Lat. Latin

lat. latitude

Latv. Latvia

L.B. *Lit(t)erarum Baccalaureus* (L.) Bachelor of Letters; Local Board

lb. *libra* (L.) pound; *librae* (L.) pounds

lb. ap. pound, apothecary's (Pharm.)

lb. av. pound avoirdupois

lbs. pounds

lb. t. pound troy

LC- landing craft (with type specified by following letter), for example, **LCI**, Landing Craft Infantry; **LCP**, Landing Craft Personnel (Mil.)

L.C. Library of Congress

L/C, l/c letter of credit

l.c. left center; *loco citato* (L.) in the place cited; lower case (Typog.)

l.c.l. less-than-carload lot (Com.)

l.c.m. least common multiple

LCT, L.C.T. local civil time

LD, LD., L.D. Low Dutch

Ld. Lord

L.Div. Licentiate in Divinity

L.D.S. Latter Day Saints, Church of Jesus Christ of (the Mormons); Licentiate in Dental Surgery

lea. league; leather

lect. lecture

L.Ed. Lawyer's edition (U.S. Supreme Court Reports)

Leg. legato (Music)

leg. legal; legate; legislative; legislature

legis. legislation; legislative; legislature

Leics. Leicestershire (England)

Leit. Leitram (Ireland)

L. ès Sc. *Licencié ès Sciences* (F.) Licentiate in Sciences

Lev., Levit. Leviticus (Biblical)

lex. lexicon

lexicog. lexicographer; lexicographical; lexicography

LF, L.F., l.f., lf low-frequency

lf. lightface (Typog.)

LG, LG., L.G. Low German (Language)

lg., lge. large

LH luteinizing hormone

LHA local hour angle (Navig.)

L.H.D. *Litteratum Humaniorum,* or *In Litteris Humanioribus, Doctor* (L.) Doctor of Humanities

Li lithium (Chem.)

li link (Chain Measure)

L.I. Long Island

Lib. Liberal (National political party in Great Britain and several other countries; statewide party in New York); Liberia

lib. *liber* (L.) book; librarian; library

Lieut. lieutenant (Mil.)

Lim. Limerick (Ireland)

lin. lineal; linear

Lincs Lincolnshire (England)

ling. linguistics

liq. liquid; liquor

lit. liter; literal; literally; literary; literature

Lit.B, Litt.B. *Lit(t)erarum Baccalaureus* (L.) Bachelor of Letters; Bachelor of Literature

Lit.D. *Literarum Doctor* (L.) Doctor of Literature

Lith. Lithuania; Lithuanian

lith., litho., lithog. lithograph; lithography

Litt.D. *Litterarum Doctor* (L.) Doctor of Letters

LL, LL. Late Latin; Low Latin

ll. lines

LL.B. *Legum Baccalaureus* (L.) Bachelor of Laws

LL.D. *Legum Doctor* (L.) Doctor of Laws

L.L.L. Love's Labour's Lost (Shak.)

L.M. Licentiate in Medicine, or in Midwifery

LMT local mean time

Lnrk. Lanark (Scotland)

loc. cit. *loco citato* (L.) in the place cited

long., lon. longitude

Long. Longford (Ireland)

L.O.O.M. Loyal Order of Moose

loq. *loquitur* (L.) he (she, it) speaks

loran long-range navigation

Lou. Louth (Ireland)

lox liquid oxygen

L-P long-playing

LPG liquefied petroleum gas

L.P.S. Lord Privy Seal

LS- landing ship (of specified type), for example, **LST,** Landing Ship Tank

L.S. Licentiate in Surgery; *locus sigilli* (L.) the place of the seal

l.s.t. local standard time

Lt lieutenant (US Mil.)

l.t. local time; long ton

Lt Col lieutenant colonel

Lt Com lieutenant commander

Ltd., ltd. limited

Lt Gen lieutenant general

Lt. Gov. lieutenant governor

L.Th. Licentiate in Theology

Lt (jg.) lieutenant (junior grade) (Mil.)

Lt. Infantry light infantry (Mil.)

Lu lutecium (Chem.)

Lucr. The Rape of Lucrece (Shak.)

Luth. Lutheran

Lux. Luxembourg

lv. leave; livre(s)

l.w.l. load waterline

l.w.m. low watermark

M

M *Mille* (L.) thousand; mobilization

M more

M. Manitoba; Monsieur; *mezzo* (Music)

M., m. majesty; male; manual; mark (Currency); marquis; married; masculine; mass; medicine; medium; meridian; *meridies* (L.) mile; mill; minim; minute; modulus; month; moon; morning

m., m meter

MA Maritime Administration

MA, M.A. mental age (Psychol.)

Ma masurium (Chem.)

ma. milliampere

M.A. *Magister Artium* (L.) Master of Arts; Military Academy

MAAG Military Assistance Advisory Group

Macb. Macbeth (Shak.)

Macc., Mac. Maccabees (Biblical)

mach. machine; machinery; machinist

Mad. Madagascar

Mad., Madm. Madam

m.a.f. moisture and ash free (coal)

mag. magazine; magnetism; magnitude (of a star)

M.Agr. Master of Agriculture

Maj Major (Mil.)

Maj Gen Major General (Mil.)

Mal. Malachi (Biblical); Malayan

Mal. Malta

Man. Manila (paper); Manitoba (Canada)

manuf. manufacture; manufactured; manufacturer; manufacturing

Mar., Mar March

mar. maritime

marc. marcato (Music)

March. Marchioness

marg. margin; marginal

Marq. Marquis

Mart. Martyrology

masc. masculine

Mass. Massachusetts

mat. matins

math. mathematical; mathematician; mathematics

MATS Military Air Transport Service

Matt. Matthew (Biblical)

max. maximum

M.B. *Medicinae Baccalaureus* (L.) Bachelor of Medicine; Militia Bureau (Mil.)

M.B.A. Master in, or of, Business Administration

M b.m. thousand (feet) board measure

MBS Mutual Broadcasting System

MC Medical Corps (US Army)

M.C. Master Commandant; Master of Ceremonies; Member of Congress

mc, mc., m.c. megacycle

M c.f. thousand cubic feet

M.C.L. Master of Civil Law

M.D. Medical Department; *Medicinae Doctor* (L.) Doctor of Medicine

Md. Maryland

M/D, m/d months' date

MDAP Mutual Defense Assistance Program (Mil.)

M.D.S. Master of Dental Surgery

mdse. merchandise

ME, ME., M.E. Middle English

Me methyl (Chem.)

Me. Maine

M.E. Methodist Episcopal; Mining, or Mechanical Engineer

m.e. marbled edges (Bookbinding)

Mea. Meath (Ireland)

meas. measure

Meas. for M. Measure for Measure (Shak.)

mech. mechanical; mechanics

M.Ed. Master of Education

med. medical; medicine; medieval; medium

Medit. Mediterranean

meg. megacycle

mem. member; memoir; memorandum; memorial

memo. memorandum

meq. milliequivalent

mer. meridian; meridional

Merch. V. The Merchant of Venice (Shak.)

Meri. Merionethshire (Wales)

Merry W. Merry Wives of Windsor (Shak.)

Messrs., Messrs Messieurs

met. metaphor; metaphysics; metropolitan

metal. metallurgy

metaph. metaphor; metaphysics

meteorol. meteorology

Meth. Methodist

meton. metonymy

Mev., Mev, mev, m.e.v. (Mev. preferred) million electron volts

Mex. Mexican; Mexico

mf. milli-farad

M.F.A. Master of Fine Arts

mfg. manufacturing

M.F.H. Master of Fox Hounds

mfr. manufacture; manufacturer

MG Military Government; machine gun (US Army)

Mg magnesium (Chem.)

mG milligauss

mg. (preferred), **mg, mgm** milligram(s)

MGB *Ministerstvo Gosudarstvennoi Bezopasnosti* (R.) Soviet Ministry of State Security, investigating treason

Mgr., Mgr Manager; Monseigneur; Monsignor

M.H. Medal of Honor (U.S.)

mh. millihenry

MHG, MHG., M.H.G. Middle High German

mi. mile; mill

M.I.C. Marian Fathers

Mic. Micah (Biblical)

M.I.C.E. Member of the Institute of Civil Engineers (N.B. see also M.I. Chem. E., etc. See above under F(ellow).)

Mich. Michael; Michigan; Michoacan (Mexico)

micros. microscopy

mid. middle; midshipman

Middlx., Midx., Mx. Middlesex (England)

Mid.L. Midlothian (Scotland)

Mids. N.D. A Midsummer Night's Dream (Shak.)

MIG, Mig *Mikoyan* and *Gurevich* (R.) Soviet jet airplane

mil, mil. military; militia

milit. military

min. mineralogical; mineralogy; minim; minimum; mining; minister; minor; minute(s)

mineral. mineralogy

Minn. Minnesota

misc. miscellaneous

Misc. Doc. (with number) miscellaneous document

Miss. Mississippi

mk. mark; markka (Fin.)

mks, m.k.s. meter-kilogram-second (system)

ml. milliliter

Mlle. Mademoiselle

Mlles. Mademoiselles

MM. Their Majesties; Messieurs (F.) Sirs

M.M. Maelzel's Metronome (Music)

mm., mm millimeter; millimeters; *millia* (L.) thousands

Mme. Madame

Mmes. Mesdames

m.m.f. magnetomotive force (Engineering)

mmfd. micromicrofarad

Mn manganese (Chem.)

M.O., MO Medical Officer; *modus operandi* (L.) method of operation (Criminology)

Mo molybdenum (Chem.)

Mo. Missouri

M.O., m.o. money order

mo. month(s)

mod. *moderato* (Music)

Moham. Mohammedan

M.O.I. Ministry of Information (Brit.)

mol. wt. molecular weight

Mon. Monaghan (Ireland) Monday; Monsignor

mon. monastery; monetary

Mong. Mongolia; Mongolian

monogr. monograph

Mon., Mons. Monmouthshire (England)

Mons. Monsieur

Monsig. Monsignor

Mont. Montana

Mont., Montgom. Montgomeryshire (Wales)

Mor. Morocco

mor. morocco

Morel. Morelos (Mexico)

morphol. morphology

MOS military occupational specialty (duty classification by number)

mos. months

Movt. movement (Music)

Moz. Mozambique

MP military police

M.P. Member of Parliament; Methodist Protestant

mp mezzo piano (Music)

m.p. melting point

M.Pd. Master of Pedagogy

M.P.E. Master of Physical Education

m.p.h., mph miles per hour

MR motivational research (Business); Moral Rearmament

Mr. Mister (Title)

M.R.A.S. Member of the Royal Academy of Sciences

MRC Metals Reserve Company

Mrs. Mistress (Title)

MS motorship

MS., Ms, ms., ms manuscript

M.S. Master of Science

m.s., M/S months after sight (Com.)

M.Sc. Master of Science

msec. millisecond

Msgr. Monsignor

MSgt, M/Sgt Master Sergeant

m.s.l. mean sea level

MSS., MSS, mss., mss manuscripts

m.s.t. mountain standard time

Ms-Th mesothorium (Chem.)

mt. megaton

m.t. metric ton; mountain time

Mt., mt. mount; mountain

mtg. meeting; mortgage

mtge. mortgage

mtn. mountain

MTO Mediterranean Theater of Operations (WWII)

MTP Mobilization Training Program (US Army)

Mt. Rev. Most Reverend

Mts., mts. mountains

mun. municipal

Much Ado Much Ado About Nothing (Shak.)

mus. museum; music; musician

Mus.B., Mus.Bac. *Musicae Baccalaureus* (L.) Bachelor of Music

Mus.D., Mus.Doc., Mus.Dr. *Musicae Doctor* (L.) Doctor of Music

mut. mutilated; mutual

MV motor vessel

m.v. mezzo voce (Music)

MVA Missouri Valley Authority

MVD *Ministerstvo Vnutrennikh Del.* (R.) Soviet Ministry of Internal Affairs, administering police, border guards, labor camps, etc.

M.W. Most Worshipful; Most Worthy

M.W.A. Modern Woodmen of America

M.W.G.M. Most Worthy Grand Master

mya. myriare

mycol. mycology

myg. myriagram

myl. myrialiter

mym. myriameter

mythol., myth. mythology

NOTES

N

N nitrogen (Chem.)

N. Nationalist; Norse; November

N., N, n. north; northern

N normal

N., n. navy; noon; normal (strength solution) (Chem.)

n. *natus* (L.) born; nephew; neuter; new; nominative; note; noun; number

Na *natrium* (L.) sodium (Chem.)

N.A. National Academician; National Army; North America

NAA, N.A.A. National Aeronautic Association

NAACP, N.A.A.C.P. National Association for the Advancement of Colored People

NAB National Association of Broadcasters

NAC national agency check

NACA National Advisory Committee for Aeronautics

N.A.D. National Academy of Design

Nah. Nahum (Biblical)

NAM National Association of Manufacturers

NASA National Aeronautics and Space Administration

nat. national

Nath. Nathaniel

nat. hist. natural history

natl. national

NATO North Atlantic Treaty Organization

NATS Naval Air Transport Service (Mil.)

naut. nautical

nav. naval; navigation

navig. navigation

Nb niobium (Chem.)

N.B. New Brunswick (Canada)

N.B., n.b. *nota bene* (L.) note well

NBA, N.B.A. National Boxing Association

NBC National Broadcasting Company

NBS National Bureau of Standards

NC Nurse Corps (Mil.)

N.C. North Carolina

N.C., n.c. nitrocellulose

NCAA, N.C.A.A. National Collegiate Athletic Association

NCO, N.C.O., n.c.o. noncommissioned officer

N.C.W.C. National Catholic Welfare Council

Nd neodymium (Chem.)

N.D. North Dakota

N.D., n.d. no date

N.Dak. North Dakota

NE., NE, N.E., n.e. northeast

Ne neon (Chem.)

N.E. New England

NEA, N.E.A. National Education Association; Newspaper Enterprise Association

Nebr. Nebraska

n.e.c. not elsewhere classified

N.E.D., NED New English Dictionary (the Oxford English Dictionary)

neg. negative; negatively

Neh. Nehemiah (Biblical)

N.E.I. Netherlands East Indies

nem. con. *nemine contradicente* (L.) without a dissenting vote; unanimously

nem. diss. *nemine dissentiente* (L.) without a dissenting vote; unanimously

NEP, Nep. New Economic Policy (R.) Russian Soviet policy (1921). Also, **nepman.** Early examples of the acronymic as described in introduction

Nep. Nepal

n.e.s. not elsewhere specified

Neth. Netherlands

Neth.Gu. Netherlands Guiana

Neth.Ind. Netherlands Indies

neut. neuter

Nev. Nevada

Newf. Newfoundland

New M. New Mexico

New Test. New Testament

N.F. National Formulary (Pharm.) Newfoundland; Norman French

N.F., n/f no funds (Banking)

n.f.e. non-ferrous extract

NG, N.G. National Guard

N.G., n.g. no good

NGr, NGr., N.Gr. New Greek

N.H. New Hampshire

NHA National Housing Agency

NHG, NHG., N.H.G. New High German

NHI National Health Insurance (Brit.)

Ni nickel (Chem.)

NIA National Intelligence Authority

Nicar. Nicaragua

Nig. Nigeria

N.J. New Jersey

NKVD, N.K.V.D. Russian Soviet secret police, successor to the Ogpu

NL, NL., N.L. New Latin

n.l. natural log or logarithm; new line (Print.); *non licet* (L.) it is not permitted or lawful; *non liquet* (L.) it is not clear

N. lat. north latitude

N.L.C.A. Norwegian Lutheran Church of America

NLRB National Labor Relations Board

N.M. New Mexico

N. Mex. New Mexico

NMI no middle initial

NNE north-northeast
NNW north-northwest

No. Noah; north; northern

No., no. *numero* (L.) by number; number

n.o.i.b.n. not otherwise indexed by name

nol. pros. *nolle prosequi* (L.) to be unwilling to prosecute (Law.)

nom. nominative

noncom. noncommissioned officer

non obst. *non obstante* (L.) notwithstanding

non pros. *non prosequitor* (L.) he will not prosecute

n.o.p. not otherwise provided for

Nor. Norman; North; Norway; Norwegian

Norf. Norfolk (England)

Northants Northamptonshire (England)

Northum(b.) Northumberland (England)

Norw. Norway

Nos., nos. numbers

n.o.s. not otherwise specified

Notts Nottinghamshire (England)

Nov. November

nov. novelist

NOVS National Office of Vital Statistics

NP neuropsychiatric

N.P. *nisi prius* (L.) unless before (used of certain actions, trials, etc.); no protest (Banking); Notary Public

Np neptunium (Chem.)

n.p. no paging (of books); no place (of publication)

NPN, N.P.N. nonprotein nitrogen

n.p. or d. no place or date

n.p.t. normal pressure and temperature

nr. near

NRA, N.R.A. National Recovery Administration

NRAB National Railroad Adjustment Board

N.R.F. *Nouvelle Revue Francaise*
N.Rh. Northern Rhodesia

NS nuclear ship

N.S. New Style (Dates according to the Gregorian Calendar); Nova Scotia (Canada)

N.S., n.s. not specified

Ns nimbo-stratus

NSA National Shipping Authority

NSC National Security Council (Mil.)

NSF National Science Foundation

N.S.P.C.A. National Society for the Prevention of Cruelty to Animals

N.S.P.C.C. National Society for the Prevention of Cruelty to Children

n.s.p.f. not specifically provided for

NSRB National Security Resources Board

N.S.W. New South Wales

Nt nitron (Chem.)

NT., N.T. New Testament

nt. wt. net weight

num. numeral; numerals

Num., Numb. Numbers (Biblical)

numis., numism. numismatic, or numismatics

NW., NW, N.W., n.w. northwest

NWC National War College (US Army)

NWLB National War Labor Board

N.W.T. Northwest Territories (Canada)

N.Y. New York

NYA National Youth Administration

Nyas. Nyasaland

N.Y.C. New York City

N.Z., N.Zeal. New Zealand

O

O oxygen (Chem.)

O. Ocean; October; Ohio (Not Official); Ontario; Order

O., o. octavo; old; order

o ohm

o- ortho. (Chem.)

o. *octarius* (L.) pint (Pharm.); off; only

OAS Organization of American States

OASI old-age and survivors insurance

Oax. Oaxaca (Mexico)

ob. obiit (L.) he (she, it) died; *obiter* (L.) in passing, i.e. incidentally; oboe

Obad. Obadiah (Biblical)

obb. obbligato (Music)

O.B.E. Officer (of the Order) of the British Empire

obj. object

obl. oblique; oblong

obs. observation; obsolete

obstet. obstetrical

obt. obedient

Oc., oc. ocean

O.C. original cover (Philately)

o.c. *opere citato* (L.) in the work cited

o/c overcharge

OCD Office of Civilian Defense

OCDM Office of Civil and Defense Mobilization

OCIAA Office of Co-ordinator of Inter-American Affairs

O.C.R. Order of Cistercian Reform, or Trappists

OCS Office of Contract Settlement; Officer Candidate School (Mil.)

Oct., Oct October

OD Officer of the Day; olive drab (Mil.)

O.D. ordinary seaman; overdraft, or overdrawn

O.D., o.d. (preferred) outside diameter

ODT Office of Defense Transportation

OE, OE., O.E. Old English

o.e. omissions excepted

O.E.D., OED Oxford English Dictionary

OEM Office for Emergency Management

O.E.S. Order of the Eastern Star

OF, OF., O.F. Old French

Off. Offaly (Ireland)

off. offered; officer; official; officinal

O.F.M. Order of Friars Minor (Franciscans)

OG Officer of the Guard (Mil.)

O.G. original gum (Philately)

Ogpu (R.) The Soviet secret police which succeeded the Cheka in 1922; called also **G.P.U.**

OHG, OHG., O.H.G. Old High German

O.H.M.S. On His (Her) Majesty's Service

OIT Office of International Trade

O.K. correct (Colloquial)

Okla. Oklahoma

Old Test. Old Testament

O.M. Order of Merit (Brit.)

ON., O.N. Old Norse

ONI Office of Naval Intelligence (Mil.)

Ont. Ontario (Canada)

OP observation post (Mil.)

O.P. Order of Preachers (Dominicans)

op. *opus* (L.) work; *opera* (L.) works (Music)

O.P., OP, o.p., op out of print; overprint (Philately); overproof

OPA Office of Price Administration

Op. Atty. Gen. Opinions of the Attorney General

op. cit. *opere citato* (L.) in the work cited

opp. opposed; opposite

opt. optative; optics

o.r. owner's risk (Transp.)

ORC Officers' Reserve Corps (Mil.)

orch. orchestra

ord. order; ordinal; ordinance; ordinary; ordnance

Orderly Sgt. orderly sergeant (GPO)

Ord. Sgt. ordnance sergeant (GPO)

Ore. Oregon

Oreg. Oregon (preferred)

org. organic; organized

orig. original; originally

Ork. Orkney (Scotland)

ornith., ornithol. ornithological; ornithology

Ortho. Greek Orthodox

OS, OS., O.S. Old Saxon

O.S. Old Style (Dates according to the Julian calendar); ordinary seaman

O.S.B. Order of St. Benedict (Benedictine)

OSD Office of the Secretary of Defense (Mil.)

OSS Office of Strategic Services

OSSR Office of Selective Service Records

O.S.U. Order of St. Ursula (Ursuline)

O.T. Old Testament

OTC Organization for Trade Cooperation

OTC, O.T.C. Officer in Tactical Command; formerly, Officers' Training Camp, or Corps (Mil.)

Oth. Othello, The Moor of Venice (Shak.)

O.U.A.M. Order of United American Mechanics

OWI Office of War Information

Oxf., Ox. Oxford

Oxf., Oxon Oxfordshire (England)

Oxon. *Oxonia* (L.) Oxford; Bishop of Oxford

oz. ounce(s)

oz. ap. ounce (apothecaries' weight)

oz. av. ounce (avoirdupois weight)

ozs. ounces

oz. t. ounce troy

P

P parental (Biol.); phosphorus (Chem.); pressure (Phys.); (prisoner (Mil.)

P., p. *pater* (L.) father; pawn (Chess; *pere* (F.) father; post: president; priest; prince; prompter (Theat.)

p. page; part; participle; past; penny; *per* (L.) by; perch (the measure); perishable; peseta (Sp.); peso (Mex.); *piano* (It.) softly (Music); pint; pole (the measure); population; *post* (L.) after; *pro* (L.) for

p- para- (Chem.)

Pa protoactinium (Chem.)

Pa. Pennsylvania

PA public address (system)

P.A. Passenger Agent; Post Adjutant; press agent; Purchasing Agent

P.A., P/A power of attorney; private account

p.a. participial adjective; per annum

PABA, paba para-aminobenzoic acid

PAC Political Action Committee

Pac. Pacific Reporter

Pac., Pacif. Pacific

Pal. Palestine

paleol. paleology

paleon. paleontology

pam., pamph. pamphlet

Pan. Panama

P. and L. profit and loss

PAPA Philippine Alien Property Administration

par. paragraph

Para. Paraguay

paren. parenthesis

parens. parentheses

parl. parliamentary

part. participle; particular

part. adj. participial adjective

pass. passenger; passive

Passed Asst. Surg. passed assistant surgeon

pat. patent; patented

patd. patented

path., pathol. pathology

Pat. Off. Patent Office

pat. pend. patent pending

P.A.U., PAU Pan American Union

P.A.Y.E. pay as you earn; pay as you enter

payt. payment

Pb *plumbum* (lead) (Chem.)

P.B. *Pharmacopoeia Britannica* (L.) British Pharmacopoeia; Plymouth Brethren; Prayer Book; Primitive Baptist

PBA Public Buildings Association

P.B.A. Patrolmen's Benevolent Association

PBS Public Buildings Service

PBX, P.B.X. private branch (telephone) exchange

PC Preparatory Commission (of the United Nations)

P.C. Past Commander; Philippine Constabulary; Police Constable; Post Commander; Privy Council, or Councilor

P/C, p/c petty cash; prices current

pc. piece; price(s)

p.c. per cent; post card

PCA Progressive Citizens of America

pct. percent

Pd palladium (Chem.)

P.D. Police Department

P.D., p.d. *per diem* (L.) by the day

pd. paid

Pd.B., Pd.D., Pd.M. Bachelor, Doctor, Master of Pedagogy

P.D.Q. pretty damn quick

P.E. Presiding Elder; probable error (Statistics); Professional Engineer; Protestant Episcopal

Ped. Pedal (Music)

ped. pedal; pedestal

Peeb. Peebles (Scotland)

P.E.I. Prince Edward Island (Canada)

Pemb. Pembrokeshire (Wales)

P.E.N. (International Association of) Poets, Playwrights, Editors, Essayists and Novelists

Pen., pen. peninsula

Penn., Penna. Pennsylvania

Pent. Pentecost

Per. Pericles, Prince of Tyre (Shak.)

per. period; person

per an., per ann. per annum

perf. perfect; perforated

perh. perhaps

perm. permanent

Pers. Persia; Persian

pers. person; personal

pert. pertaining

Peruv. Peruvian

Pet. Peter (Biblical)

Pet. Peters (US Supreme Court Reports)

petrog. petrography

petrol. petrology

pF water energy (**p.** logarithm; **F.** frequency)

pf. pfennig (Ger. mon. unit); preferred

Pfc private first class (Mil.)

pfd. preferred

pfg. pfennig

Pg. Portugal; Portugese

P.G. Past Grand; postgraduate

PGA Professional Golfers Association

P.H. Purple Heart

pH hydrogen-ion concentration

Ph phenyl (Chem.)

ph. phase

PHA Public Housing Administration

Phar.B., Phar.D., Phar.M. Bachelor, Doctor, Master of Pharmacy

Pharm., Phar. pharmaceutical; pharmacopoeia; pharmacy

Ph.B. Bachelor of Philosophy

Ph.C. Pharmaceutical Chemist

Ph.D. Doctor of Philosophy

Ph. G. graduate in pharmacy

Phil. Philip; Philippians (Biblical); Philippine

phil. philosophy

Phila. Philadelphia

Philem. Philemon (Biblical)

Phil. I., Phil. Is. Philippine Islands

philol. philology

philos. philosophy

Phoen. The Phoenix and the Turtle (Shak.)

phon., phonet. phonetics

photo. photograph

photog. photography

photom. photometry

phr. phrase

phren., phrenol. phrenology

PHS Public Health Service

phys. physical; physician; physics

physiol. physiological; physiology

P.I. Philippine Islands

Pi., pias. piaster

PICAO Provisional International Civil Aviation Organization

Pilg. The Passionate Pilgrim (Shak.)

pinx. pinxit (L.) he (she) painted it

P.J.'s pajamas (Slang)

pk. pack; park; peak; peck

pkg., pkge. package, or packages

pkt. packet

P.L. Poet Laureate

Pl. place

pl. plate; plural

plat platoon (Mil.)

plu. plural

plupf. pluperfect

plur. plural; plurality

PM Provost Marshal (Mil.)

PM. Paymaster; Postmaster

P.M. Past Master; Police Magistrate

P.M., p.m. (preferred) post meridiem

p.m. post-mortem

PMA Production and Marketing Administration

P.M.G. Postmaster General

pmk postmark

pmkd postmarked

p.n., P/N promissory note

pneum. pneumatic

pnxt. pinxit

PO petty officer (Mil.)

Po polonium (Chem.)

P.O., p.o. petty officer; postal order; post office

po, p.o. put-out (Baseball)

P.O.D. Post Office Department

p.o.d. pay on delivery

Pod.D. Doctor of Podiatry

poet. poetic; poetical; poetry

P. of H. Patrons of Husbandry

Pol. Poland; Polish

pol. econ., polit. econ. political economy

Polit. political; politics

pop. popularity; population

pop. popularly; population

p.o.r. pay on return

Port. Portugal; Portegese

pos. positive; possessive

poss. possession; possessive; possible; possibly

pot. potential

POW prisoner of war

PP pellagra preventive (factor)

P.P., p.p. parcel post; parish priest; past participle; postpaid

pp. pages; privately printed

pp. pianissimo (Music)

ppd. postpaid; prepaid

pph. pamphlet

PPI plan position indicator

p.p.i. policy proof of interest

p.p.m. part(s) per million

ppp. pianississimo (Music)

p.pr., ppr. participle present

P.P.S., p.p.s. *post-postscriptem* (L.) an additional postscript

P.Q. Province of Quebec

p.q. previous question

Pr praseodymium (Chem.)

Pr. Provencal

Pr., pr. preferred (stock)

P.R. press release; proportional representation; public relations; Puerto Rico

pr. pair; pairs; paper; power; present; price; priest; prince; printing; pronoun

PRA Public Roads Administration

prec. preceding

precanc. precanceled

pred. predicate

pref. preface; preference; preferred; prefix

prelim. preliminary

prep. preparation; preparatory; prepare; preposition

Pres. President

pres. present; presidency

Presb. Presbyterian

pret. preterit

prim. primary; primitive

prin. principal; principally; principle

print. printing

Private Res. (with number) private resolution

P.R.O. public relations officer (Mil.)

prob. probably; problem

proc. proceedings; process
prod. produced

Prof., prof. professor

prom. promontory

pron. pronominal; pronoun; pronounced; pronunciation

prop. properly; property; proposition

propr. proprietor

pros. posody

Prot. Protestant

pro tem. *pro tempore* (L.) temporarily (In the absence of the Vice President, the majority leader becomes president *pro tem.* of the U.S. Senate.)

Prov. Provencal; Proverbs (Biblical)

prov. province; provincial; provisional; provost

prs. pairs

Prus., Pruss. Prussia; Prussian

P.S. Privy Seal; public sale; Public School

P.S., p.s. passenger steamer; permanent secretary; *post scriptum* (L.) postscript

Ps., Psa. Psalm; Psalms (Biblical)

ps. pieces

pseud. pseudonym

p.s.f., psf pounds per square foot

p.s.i. pounds per square inch

P.SS. *postscripta* (L.) postscripts

P.s.t., PST, P.S.T. Pacific Standard Time

psych., psychol. psychological; psychology

Pt platinum (Chem.)

pt. part; pint

P.T.A. Parent-Teacher Association

pta. peseta

PT boat patrol torpedo boat (USN)

Pte. Private (Brit.)

Ptg., ptg. printing

p.t.o. please turn over

pty. ltd. proprietary limited

Pu plutonium (Chem.)

pub. public; published; publisher; publishing

Public Res. (with number) public resolution

Pueb. Puebla (Mexico)

Pvt private (US Army)

PW Prisoner of War; *Publishers' Weekly*

PWA Public Works Administration

P.W.D., PWD Public Works Department

pwt. pennyweight

PX post exchange (Mil.)

pxt. *pinxit* (L.) he painted it

Q

Q. Quebec

Q., q. quarto; question

q. *quadrans* (L.) farthing; quart; quarter (of a hundredweight); quarterly; quasi; queen; query; quetzal (Guat.); quintal; quire

QB queen's bishop (Chess)

Q.B. Queen's Bench

Q.C. Queen's Council

Q.E.D. *quod erat demonstrandum* (L.) which was to be demonstrated

Q.F. quick-firing

QKt Queen's Knight

ql. quintal

QM quartermaster

QMC Quartermaster Corps

QM Gen, Q.M. Gen. Quartermaster General (Mil.) (GPO)

QM Sgt, Q.M. Sgt. quartermaster sergeant (Mil.) (GPO)

Q.P., q.pl. *quantum placet* (L.) as much as you please

Qq quartos

qq. questions

qr. *quadrans* (L.) farthing; quarter; quire (Paper)

qt. quantity; quart; quarts

Q.T., q.t. quiet; usually, on the q.t.

qto. quarto

qu., quar., quart. quarter; quarterly

Que. Quebec (Canada)

Quer. Querétaro (Mexico)

ques. question

quot. quotation

q.v. *quod vide* (L.) which see

R

R radical, esp. hydrocarbon radical (Chem.); radius; ratio (Math.); rook (Chess); gas constant (Phys. Chem.)

R, r resistance (Elec.); royal; ruble
R. Réaumur; Republican; respond, or response (Church Service); ring (Org. Chem.)

R., r. rabbi; railroad; railway; rector; redactor; regina; rex; right; river; road; royal; rupee

r roentgen(s)

r. rare; received (Com.); recipe; resides; retired; right; rises; rod; rook (Chess); rubber; ruble

Ra radium (Chem.)

RA Regular Army (US)

R.A. right ascension (Astron.); Royal Academy, or Academician; Royal Artillery

R.A.A.F. Royal Australian Air Force

Rab. Rabbi; rabbinate

rabb. rabbinical

RACON, racon radar beacon (US Army) (GPO)

Rad. Radnorshire (Wales)

rad. radical; radix

radar radio detection and ranging

RAdm Rear Admiral

R.A.F. Royal Air Force

rall. *rallentando* (Music)

R.A.M. Royal Academy of Music

Rand Corp. (research and development) (US Govt.)

rato rocket-assisted takeoff

RB Renegotiation Board

Rb rubidium (Chem.)

RBI, r.b.i. run(s) batted in (Baseball)

R.C., RC Red Cross; Roman Catholic

R.C.A.F. Royal Canadian Air Force

R.C.Ch. Roman Catholic Church

Rct recruit (US Army)

RD Radarman (USN)

R.D. Rural Delivery

R/D refer to drawer (Banking)

Rd., rd. rix-dollar, a silver coin of German, Dutch or Scand. minting, worth generally $1.00; road

rd. rod; round

RDB Research and Development Board

R.E. Right Excellent; Royal Engineers

Re. rupee

REA Rural Electrification Administration

Rear Adm. Rear Admiral

Réaum. Réaumur

rec. receipt; recipe; record; recorded; recorder

recd. received

Recit. Recitative (Music)

rec. sec. recording secretary

Rect. Rector; Rectory

rect. receipt; rector; rectory

Ref. Reformation

ref. referee; reference; referred; reformed; refunding

Ref.Ch. Reformed Church

refl. reflection; reflective; reflectively; reflex; reflexive

Ref. Pres. Reformed Presbyterian

Ref. Sp. Reformed Spelling

reg. regent; regiment; region; registrar; registered; registry; regular; regularly; regulation; regulator

regt. regent; regiment

rel. relating; relative; relatively; religion; religious

rel. pron. relative pronoun

Renf. Renfrew (Scotland)

Rep. Representative; Republican

rep. report; reporter; representative; republic

r.e.p. roentgen equivalent physical

repr. representing; reprinted

Repub. Republic; Republican

req. required; requisition

res. reserve; residence; resides; resigned

resp. respective; respectively; respiration; respondent

restr. restaurant

Resurr. Resurrection

ret. retired; returned

Rev. Stat. Revised Statutes

retd. retained; returned

Rev. Revelation (Biblical); Reverand

rev. revenue; reverse; review; reviewed; revise; revised; revision; revolution; revolving

Rev. Ver. Revised Version (of the Bible)

RF radiofrequency

R.F., r.f. radio frequency; rapid-fire

rf., rfz. *rinforzando* (Music)

R.F.A. Royal Field Artillery

RFC Reconstruction Finance Corporation

R.F.C. Royal Flying Cross

R.F.D. Rural Free Delivery
Rh Rhesus (blood factor); rhodium (Chem.)

R.H. Royal Highness

r.h. relative humidity

rheo. rheostat, or rheostats

rhet. rhetoric; rhetorical

R.I. Rhode Island

Rich. Richard

Rich. II The Life and Death of King Richard II (Shak.)

Rich. III The Life and Death of King Richard III (Shak.)

R.I.I.A. Royal Institute of International Affairs

rinf. *rinforzando* (Music)

R.I.P. *requiesca(n)t in pace* (L.) may he or she (or they) rest in peace

Ritard. *ritardando* (Music)

rinf. *rinforzando* (Music)

riv. river

RJ road junction

RM, r.m. reichsmark(s)

rm. ream (Paper)

R.M.A. Royal Military Academy (Woolwich)

R.M.C. Royal Military College (Sandhurst)

rms. rooms

rms, r.m.s. root mean square

R.M.S. Royal Mail service, or Steamship

Rn radon (Chem.)

R.N. Registered Nurse; Royal Navy

R.N.R. Royal Naval Reserve

R.N.V.R. Royal Naval Volunteer Reserve

R.N.Z.A.F. Royal New Zealand Air Force

ro. rector; roan; rood

Rob., Robt. Robert

ROK Republic of Korea (Geog.)

Rom. Roman; Romance; Romania; Romanian; Romans (Biblical)

Rom. Cath. Roman Catholic

Rom. & Jul. Romeo and Juliet (Shak.)

ROP run of paper (Advertising)

Ros. Roscommon (Ireland)

Ross. Ross & Cromarty (Scotland)

rot. rotating; rotation

ROTC, R.O.T.C. Reserve Officers' Training Corps

roul. roulette (Philately)

Roum. Roumania; Roumanian

Rox. Roxburgh (Scotland)

R.P. Regius Professor

R.P.I. Rensselaer Polytechnic Institute

rpm, r.p.m. revolutions per minute

R.P.O. Railway Post Office

r.p.s. revolutions per second

rpt. report

R.Q. respiratory quotient

RR. railroad

R.R. railroad; Right Reverend

RRB Railroad Retirement Board

Rs, rs. rupees

R.S. Revised Statutes

R.S.F.S.R., RSFSR Russian Socialist Federated Soviet Republic

R.S.V.P., r.s.v.p. *Répondez, s'il vous plaît* (F.) please reply

rt. right

Rt. Hon. Right Honorable

Rt. Rev. Right Reverend

Rts. rights (Stocks & Bonds)

Ru ruthenium (Chem.)

rub. ruble

Rum. Rumania; Rumanian

Rus., Russ. Russia; Russian

Rut., Rutd., Rutl. Rutlandshire (England)

R.V. Revised Version (of the Bible)

R.W. Right Worshipful, or Worthy

Rx. recipe

Ry. railway

S

S sulfur (Chem.)

S., S, s south

S. Senate bill (with number)

S. Sabbath; Saint; Saturday; Saxon; Seaman; *senza* (Music); September; Signor; Sunday

s. sacral (Anat.); second; section; see; semi-; series; set; shilling; sign; signed; silver; singular; sire (Pedigree); solo; son; sou; steamer; stem; substantive; sucre; sun; surplus

S., s. saint; school; scribe; senate; socialist; society; soprano (Music); southern; steel

s- symmetrical (Chem.)

S1, S2, S3, S4 S1, Adjutant; S2, Intelligence Officer; S3, Operations & Training Officer; S4, Supply Officer (US Army)

Sa samarium (Chem.)

SA seaman apprentice (USN)

SA, S.A. *Sturmabteilung* (G.) literally, storm section, abbrev. for Hitler's brown-shirted private army of thugs, the storm troopers

S.A. Salvation Army; sex appeal (Slang); *Societé Anonyme* (Business); South Africa; South America; South Australia

s.a. *sine anno* (L.) without year; semiannual

Sab. Sabbath

SAC Strategic Air Command

SACEUR Supreme Allied Commander Europe

SAE, S.A.E. Society of Automotive Engineers

S.Afr., S. Afr. South Africa

SAGE semiautomatic ground environment

Salop Shropshire (England)

Salv. Salvador, also El Salvador

S.Am., S. Amer. South America; South American

Sam. Samaritan; Samoa

Sam., Saml. Samuel (Biblical)

Sans., Sansk. Sanskrit

s. and s.c. sized and supercalandered

s.ap. scruple (apothecaries' weight)

S.A.R. Sons of the American Revolution

Sard. Sardinia

Sask. Saskatchewan (Canada)

Sat. Saturday; Saturn

Sau.Ar. Saudi Arabia

Sax. Saxon; Saxony

S.B., S.D., S.M. Bachelor, Doctor, Master of Science

Sb *stibium* (L.) antimony

sb. substantive

s.b. stolen base

SBA Small Business Administration

SC Security Council (of the UN)

Sc scandium (Chem.); strato-cumulus (Meteor.)

Sc. science; Scotch; Scots; Scottish

S.C. Sanitary Corps; South Carolina; Supreme Court

sc. scale; scene; science; scilicet; screw; scruple

s.c. small capitals (Print.); supercalandered

Scan., Scand. Scandinavia

SCAP Supreme Commander for the Allied Powers (Japan)

Sc.D. *Scientiae Doctor* (L.) Doctor of Science

Scher. *scherzo,* or *scherzando* (Music)

S. Con. Res. (with number) Senate concurrent resolution

Scot. Scotch; Scotland; Scottish

scr. scruple

Script. Scripture; scriptural

SCS Soil Conservation Service

sc., sculps. *sculpsit* (L.) he (she) carved it

sculp., sculpt. sculptor; sculptural; sculpture

S.C.V. Sons of Confederate Veterans

S.D., s.d. standard deviation

s.d. *sine die* (L.) without date

S.D.A. Seventh Day Adventists

S. Dak. South Dakota

S. Doc. (with number) Senate document

SE, SE, S.E., s.e. southeast

Se selenium (Chem.)

Seabee Construction Battalion (USN) a civilian volunteer in the Civil Engineers Corps in WW II

SEATO Southeast Asia Treaty Organization

SEC Securities and Exchange Commission

sec secant

sec. second; secondary; seconds; secretary; section; sections; sector

sec.-ft. second-foot

sech hyperbolic secant

2d, 3d second, third

2d Lt second lieutenant

S1c. seaman, first class

secs. seconds; sections

sect. section

secy. secretary

Seg. *segue* (Music)

seismol. seismology

sel. selected; selections

Selk. Selkirk (Scotland)

Sem. Seminary; Semitic

Sem., Semp. *sempre* (Music)

Sen., sen. senate; senator; senior

Sep. Septuagint

sep. sepal; separate

Sept., Sept September

seq. sequel

seq. seqq. *sequential* (L.) the following

ser. series; sermon

Serb. Serbia; Serbian

Serg., Sergt. sergeant

serv. servant; service

Sf. Svedberg flotation

sf., sfz. *sforzando* (Music)

SFC sergeant, first class (US Army)

sg, s.g. senior grade

s.g. specific gravity

sgd. signed

Sgt. sergeant

sh. share; sheep (Bookbinding); sheet; shilling, or shillings

SHA sidereal hour angle (Navigation)

SHAEF Supreme Headquarters, Allied Expeditionary Forces

Shak. Shakespeare

SHAPE Supreme Headquarters Allied Powers (Europe)

Shet. Shetland (Scotland)

SHF superhigh frequency

shoran short range (radio)

s. hp. shaft horsepower

shpt. shipment

shr. share; shares

shtg. shortage

S.I. Sandwich Islands; Staten Island (N.Y.)

Si silicon (Chem.)

Sib. Siberia; Siberian

Sic. Sicilian; Sicily

Sig., sig. signature; signor; signore; signori

sigill *sigillum* (L.) seal

sim. similar

sin sine

Sin. Sinaloa (Mexico)

sing. singular

sinh hyperbolic sine

S.J. Society of Jesus; the Jesuit Fathers

S.J.D. *Scientiae Juridicae Doctor* (L.) Doctor of Juridical Science

S.J. Res. (with number) Senate joint resolution

sk. sack

Skr. Sanskrit; also **Skt.**

S. lat. south latitude

Slav. Slavic; Slavonian

sld. sailed; sealed

S.L.P. San Luis Potosi (Mexico)

Sm samarium (Chem.)

S.M. *Scientiae Magister* (L.) Master of Science; Soldier's Medal; State Militia

S.M.O.M. Sovereign and Military Order of Malta. The smallest country in the world, located in downtown Rome.

S. Mar. San Marino

sm.c., sm. caps small capitals

SN Seaman (USN)

Sn stannum (Chem.)

Sn. sanitary

So sonarman (USN)

So. south; southern

s.o. seller's option

s.o.b. son of a bitch

Soc., soc. society

sociol. sociology

sofar sound fixing and ranging

S. of S. Song of Solomon

Sol. Solicitor; Solomon

sol. soluble; solution

Som., Somerset Somersetshire (England)

Son. Sonora (Mexico)

sonar sound, navigation and ranging

Sonn. Sonnets (Shak.)

SOP standard operating procedure

sop. soprano

SP self-propelled; shore patrol, or police (USN)

Sp. Spain; Spaniard; Spanish

sp. special; species; specific; specimen; spelling; spirit

SP 4,5,6,7,8,9 Specialists 4,5,6,7,8 & 9 (US Army)

Sp3c. specialist, third class (USN)

s.p. *sine prole* (L.) without issue; supraprotest

SPARS (from Coast Guard motto "*Semper Peratus*—Always Ready") Women's Coast Guard Reserves

S.P.A.S. *Societatis Philosophicae Americanae Socius* (L.) Member of the American Philosophical Society

S.P.C.A. Society for the Prevention of Cruelty to Animals

S.P.C.C. Society for the Prevention of Cruelty to Children

spec. special; specification; speculation (usually used as in "on spec"); spectacular (U.S. TV)

specif. specifically

sp. gr. specific gravity

sp. ht. specific heat

spp. species (pl.)

SPQR *Senatus Populusque Romanus* (L.) the Senate and People of Rome. One of the granddaddies of all abbreviations.

S.P.R. Society for Psychical Research.

spt. seaport

sq squadron (Mil.)

Sq. square (street)

sq. square; sequence; *sequentia* (L.) the following; also in compounds, as sq. ft., sq. in., etc.

sqd squad (Mil.)

SR Seaman Recruit (USN)

Sr strontium (Chem.)

Sr. Senior; Señor; Sir; Sister

S.R. Sons of the Revolution

Sra. Señora

S. Rept. (with number) Senate report

S.R.O. standing room only

Srta. Señorita

SS, S.S. *Schutzstaffel* (G.) Hitler's black-uniformed Elite Guard of fanatical Nazis, ultimately formed into army divisions for WW II

SS, S.S., S/S steamship

SS. *Sancti* (L.) Saints; Saints

S.S. Silver Star; Sunday School; *supra scriptum* (L.) written above

SSA Social Security Administration

SSE south-southeast

S.S.F. standard Saybolt furol

SSgt staff sergeant

SSR, S.S.R. Soviet Socialist Republic

SSS Selective Service System

S.S.U. standard Saybolt universal

SSW south-southwest

St stratus

St. Saint; Strait; stratus; Street

St., st. statute; statutes

st. stanza; stere; stet; stitch; stone (weight); strophe

Stat. Statutes at Large

s.t. short ton

Sta. Santa; Station

sta. stationary; stator

Staff. Staffordshire (England)

stat. statuary; statue; statute (miles); statutes

S.T.B. *Sacrae Theologiae Baccalaureus* (L.) Bachelor of Sacred Theology

S.T.D. *Sacrae Theologiae Doctor* (L.) Doctor of Sacred Theology; *Scientiae Theologicae Doctor* (L.) Doctor of Theology

std. c.f. standard cubic foot (feet)

Ste. *Sainte* (F.) fem. of Saint; Stephen

ster., stg. sterling

stereo. stereotype

St. Ex. Stock Exchange

stg. sterling

stge. storage

Stir. Stirling (Scotland)

stk. stock

str. steamer; string, or strings (Music)

String. *stringendo* (Music)

stud. student

sub. subaltern; submarine; substitute; suburb; suburban

subch. subchapter

subj. subject; subjective; subjectively; subjunctive

subpar. subparagraph

subsec. subsection

subst. substantive; substitute

suf. suff. suffix

Suff. Suffolk (England)

Sun., Sund. Sunday

SUNFED Special United Nations Fund for Economic Development

sup. superior; superlative; supplement; supplementary; supply; *supra* (L.) above; supreme

Sup. Ct. Supreme Court Reporter

super. superfine; superior

superl. superlative

supp., suppl. supplement

Supp. Rev. Stat. Supplement to the Revised Statutes

supr. supreme

Supt., supt. superintendent

Sur. Surrey (England)

sur. surcharged; surplus

Surg., surg. surgeon

surg. surgeon; surgery

Surg. Gen. Surgeon General

surv. survey; surveying; surveyor

Sus. Susanna (Biblical); Sussex (England)

Suth. Sutherland (Scotland)

s.v. *sub verbo,* or *sub voce* (L.) under the word

SW., SW, S.W., s.w. southwest; southwestern

Sw., Swed. Sweden; Swedish

SW (2d) Southwestern Reporter, second series

Switz., Swit., Swtz. Switzerland

sym-, sym. symmetrical (Chem.)

sym. symbol; symphony

syn. synonym; synonymy

synd. syndicated

synop. synopsis

Syr. Syria

syr. syrup (Pharm.)

syst. system

T

T tantalum (Chem.); temperature (on the absolute scale); (surface) tension; tritium

T. *Tenore* (It.) tenor (Music) Testament; Tuesday; Turkish

t. tare; target; telephone; temperature; tempo (Music); *tempore* (L.) in the time of; tenor; tense (Gram.); territorial; territory; thaler or talari (money, Ethiopia); time; tome; ton, or tons; *tonneau* (F.) (metric) ton; town; township; transit; transitive; troy (wt.)

T- triple bond (Chem.)

Ta tantalum (Chem.)

tab. tables

tal. qual. *talis qualis* (L.) as they come; average quality

Tam. Tamaulipas (Mexico)

Tam. Shr. The Taming of the Shrew (Shak.)

tan, tan. tangent

Tan. Tanganyika

tanh hyperbolic tangent

Tas. Tasmania

Tass, TASS *Telegraphnoye Agentstvo Sovyetskovo Soyuza* (Russ.) the Soviet News Agency

TB, T.B., Tb, t.b. tubercle bacillus; tuberculosis

Tb terbium (Chem.)

t.b. trial balance

tbsp., tbs. tablespoon

TC Trustee Council (of the United Nations)

Tc technetium

tc. tierce; tierces

TCCA Textile Color Card Association (of the U.S.)

TCS traffic control station

TD tank destroyer (WW II); touchdown; Tradevman (i.e., training devices man) (USN)

T.D. Treasury Decisions

T.D.N., t.d.n. totally digestible nutrients

Te tellurium (Chem.)

tech. technical; technology

technol. technology

Tech. Sgt. Technical Sergeant (US Army, WW II)

tel. telegram; telegraph; telegraphic; telephone

teleg. telegram; telegraph; telegraphic; telephone

Temp. The Tempest (Shak.)

temp. temperature; temporary; *tempore* (L.) in the time of

ten. tenor

ten. *tenuto* (Music)

Tenn. Tennessee

Ter. terrace

ter. terrace; territory

term. terminal; termination

terr. terrace; territorial; territory

Test. Testament

Teut. Teuton; Teutonic

Tex. Texan; Texas

text rec. *textus receptus* (L.) the received text

tfr. transfer (Finance)

t.g. type genus

Th thorium (Chem.)

Th. Thomas; Thursday

T.H. Territory of Hawaii (granted statehood 1958)

Thad. Thaddeus

Thai. Thailand (formerly Siam)

Th.D. *Theologiae Doctor* (L.) Doctor of Theology

theat. theatrical

Th-Em thoron (Chem.)

Theo. Theodore; Theodosia

theol. theologian; theological; theology

theor. theorem

theos. theosophical; theosophy

therm. thermometer

Thess. Thessalonians

Tho., Thos. Thomas

3-D three-dimensional (effect) (Photography)

Thurs., Thur. Thursday

Ti titanium (Chem.)

Tib. Tibet

Tim. Timothy (Biblical)

Timon Timon of Athens (Shak.)

tinct. tincture

Tip. Tipperary (Ireland)

Tit. Titus (Biblical)

tit. title

Tit. A. Titus Andronicus (Shak.)

tk. truck

TKO, t.k.o. technical knockout (Pugilism), when the referee stops a fight without a ten-count, usually to spare a boxer from further punishment

Tl thallium (Chem.)

Tlax. Tlaxacala (Mexico)

t.l.o. total loss only

t.m. true mean

Tm thulium (Chem.)

T Mort trench mortar

Tn thoron (Chem.)

tn. ton; train

tng. training

TNT, T.N.T. trinitrotoluene; trinitrotoluol

t.o. turn over

Tob. Tobit (Biblical)

tonn. tonnage

top. topographical

topog. topography; -ical

tox., toxicol. toxicology

Tp., tp. township

t.p. title page

Tps., tps. townships

Tr terbium (Chem.)

tr. transitive; translated; translation; translator; transpose; treasurer

trag. tragedy

Tr. & Cr. Troilus and Cressida (Shak.)

trans. transactions; transferred; transitive; translated; translation; translator; transportation; transpose; transverse

transf, transferred

transp. transportation

trav. traveler; travels

treas. treasurer; treasury

treasr. treasurer

trem. tremolando (Music)

t.r.f., t-r-f, T.R.F. tuned radio frequency

trfd. transferred

trig., trigon. trigonometrical; trigonometry

Trin. Trinitarian; Trinity

trit. triturate

trop. tropic; tropical

trp troop (Mil.)

TS Top Secret (Mil.)

T.S. WW II military slang. Euphemistically, abbrev. for **tough sledding;** also an adjective, as in advising other servicemen to "get your T.S. card punched by the Chaplain."

T2g technician, second grade

tsp. teaspoon

T.T. Tanganyika Territory

Tu thulium; tungsten

T.U.C. Trades Union Congress (Brit.)

Tues., Tu. Tuesday

Tun. Tunisia

Turk. Turkey; Turkish

TV television

TVA Tennessee Valley Authority

Twad. Twaddell

2,4-D insecticide

Twel. N. Twelfth Night; or, What You Will (Shak.)

Two Gent. Two Gentlemen of Verona (Shak.)

Ty. Territory

typ., typo., typog. typographer; typographic; typographical; typography

Tyr. Tyrone (Ireland)

U

U uranium (Chem.)

u. una (Music); *und* (G.) and

U., u. uncle; university; upper

U.A.R. United Arab Republic

UAW, U.A.W. United Auto, Aircraft and Agricultural Implements Workers

U.B. United Brethren

uc. uppercase (Printing)

u.c. una corda (Music)

U.C.V. United Confederate Veterans (U.S.)

U.D.C. United Daughters of the Confederacy (U.S.)

U.F.C. United Free Church (of Scotland)

Ug. Uganda

UHF, U.H.F., u.h.f. ultra-high frequency, of a frequency between 300 and 3,000 megacycles per second (see VHF)

U.J.A. United Jewish Appeal

U.K. United Kingdom (of Great Britain and Northern Ireland)

Ukr. Ukraine

ult. ultimate; ultimately

ult., ulto. *ultimo* (L.) in the last month

UM underwater mechanic (USN)

UMTS Universal Military Training Service (or System)

U.M.W., UMW United Mine Workers

UN United Nations (originally UNO)

UNCIO United Nations Conference on International Organization

UNESCO United Nations Educational, Scientific, and Cultural Organization

UNICEF United Nations Children's Fund

Unit. Unitarian; Unitarianism

Univ. Universalist

univ. universal; universally; university

UNRRA United Nations Relief and Rehabilitation Administration

U. of S. Afr. Union of South Africa

U.P. United Presbyterian

UPI United Press International

up. upper

Ur uranium (Chem.)

Uru. Uruguay

U.S., US United States

U.S. U.S. Supreme Court Reports

u.s. *ubi supra* (L.) in the place above mentioned; *ut supra* (L.) as above

U.S.A. Union of South Africa; United States of America

USA United States Army

USAF United States Air Force

USAFI United States Armed Forces Institute

U.S.Afr., U. of S. Afr. Union of South Africa

USAR United States Army Reserve

USAREUR U.S. Army, Europe

U.S.C. United States Code

U.S.C.A. United States Code Annotated

USCC United States Commercial Company

U.S.C. Supp. United States Code Supplement

USCG United States Coast Guard

USDA United States Department of Agriculture

USES U.S. Employment Service

U.S. 40, U.S. No. 40 U.S. Highway No. 40

USIA United States Information Agency

U.S.M. United States Mail

USMA United States Military Academy

USMC United States Marine Corps

USN U.S. Navy

USNA United States Naval Academy

USNG, U.S.N.G. United States National Guard

USNR United States Naval Reserve

USO United Service Organizations

U.S.P. United States Pharmacopoeia

U.S.S. U.S. Senate; U.S. Ship

U.S.S.R. Union of Soviet Socialist Republics

usu. usual; usually

U.S.V. United States Volunteers

usw. *und so weiter* (G.) and so forth

Ut. Utah (Not Official)

u.t. universal time

ut. dict. *ut dictum* (L.) as directed

V

V five; vanadium (Chem.) vector (Math.); velocity; victory

V, v volt; volume

V. Venerable; Vicar; Virgin; Viscount

v. valve; ventral; verb; verse; version; versus; vice-; vide; village; vocative; voce; voice; volt; voltage; volume; volunteers; *von* (G.) of (in names)

VA Veterans' Administration

Va. Virginia

V.A. Vicar Apostolic; Vice-Admiral; (order of) Victoria and Albert

v.a. verb active

VAR visual-aural range

var. variant; variation; variety; variometer; various

Vat. Vatican

v. aux. verb auxiliary

vb. verb

vb. n. verb noun

VC Veterinary Corps

V.C. Vice-Chancellor; Vice-Consul; Victoria Cross

V.D. venereal disease

v.d. various dates

V-Day Victory day, originally signifying the day of Nazi Germany's defeat in Europe, and later adapted for the day of victory over Japan (V-J Day)

V-E Day Victory in Europe, May 8, 1945, the date of Nazi Germany surrender

vel. vellum

Ven. Venerable; Venice

Ven. & Ad. Venus and Adonis (Shak.)

Venez. Venezuela

Ver. Vera Cruz (Mexico)

ver. verse or verses

verb sap. *verbum satis sapienti* (L.) a word to the wise is sufficient

Vet., vet. veteran; veterinarian; veterinary

veter. veterinary

VFW, V.F.W. Veterans of Foreign Wars

VHF, V.H.F., vhf very high frequency, between 30,000 kilocycles and 300 megacycles. (Almost all U.S. TV stations use VHF.)

Vi virginium (Chem.)

V.I. Virgin Islands

Vic. Vicar; Vicarage

Vic., Vict. Victoria

Vice Adm. Vice Admiral; also, VAdm (USN)

Vict. Victoria (Australia)

vid. vide

vil. village

v. imp. verb impersonal

VIP, V.I.P. very important person (Informal)

Virg. Virgin

Vis., Visc., Visct. Viscount

V-J Day Victory over Japan, August 14, 1945, the date of Japan's surrender, WW II

VLF very low frequency

V.M.D. *Veterinariae Medicinae Doctor* (L.) Doctor of Veterinary Medicine

v.n. verb neuter

voc. vocative

vocab. vocabulary

VOL Volunteer Officer (US Army)

vol. volcano; volume

vols. volumes

vox pop. *vox populi* (L.) voice of the people

V.P. Vice President

v.p. various places

V.Rev. Very Reverend

v.s. *vide supra* (L.) see above; *volti subito* (Music)

vs. versus; also *v.*

V.S. Veterinary Surgeon

VSS. versions

Vt. Vermont

v.t. verb transitive

VT fuze variable timing fuze

Vulg. Vulgate (version of the Bible)

vulg. vulgar; vulgarly

v.v. verses; vice versa; violins

V.W. Very Worshipful

W

W, w watt

W *wolfram* (G.) tungsten (Chem.)

W. Wales; Warden; Washington; Wednesday; Welsh

W., W, w. west

W., w. warden; warehousing; weight; western; width; won; work (Physics)

w. wanting; watt; week, or weeks; wide; wife; with

W.A. West Africa; Western Australia

WAA War Assets Administration

WAAC Women's Army Auxiliary Corps

WAAF Women's Auxiliary Air Force (Brit.)

WAAS Women's Auxiliary Army Service (Brit.)

WAC Women's Army Corps; a Wac (U.S.)

WAF Women in the Air Force; a Waf (U.S.)

WAFS Women's Auxiliary Ferrying Squadron (US Army)

Wal. Walloon

Wal., Walach. Walachian

Wall. Wallace (U.S. Supreme Court Reports)

War Warwickshire (England)

Wash. Washington

WASP Women's Air Force Service Pilots

Wat. Waterford (England)

watt-hr. watt-hour

WAVES Women Accepted for Volunteer Emergency Service; a Wave (USN)

W.b., W/b waybill

w.b. warehouse book; water ballast; westbound

W.C. Wesleyan Chapel

w.c. water closet

W.C.T.U. Woman's Christian Temperance Union

WD, W.D. War Department

Wed. Wednesday

Westm. Westminster; Westmorland (England); Westmeath (Ireland)

Wex. Wexford (Ireland)

wf, w.f. wrong font (Printing)

WFTU World Federation of Trade Unions

W. Ger. West Germanic

wh., whr. watt-hour

Wheat. Wheaton (U.S. Supreme Court Reports)

whf. wharf

WHO World Health Organization

w.-hr. watt-hour

W.I. West Indies

w.i. when issued (Stocks)

Wig. Wigtown (Scotland)

Wilts. Wiltshire (England)

Wint. T. The Winter's Tale (Shak.)

Wis., Wisc. Wisconsin

Wisd. Wisdom (Book of); Wisdom of Solomon (Biblical)

wk. week; work

wks. weeks; works

W.L. West Lothian (Scotland)

WL, w.l. water line; wave length

WLB War Labor Board

W. long. west longitude

Wm. William

W.M. Worshipful Master

WMC War Manpower Commission

wmk. watermark

WNW west-northwest

WO, W.O. wait order; Warrant Officer

w.o.c. without compensation

WO (jg.) warrant officer (junior grade)

Worcs Worcestershire (England)

W.P. Worthy Patriarch

WPA Works Progress Administration

WPB War Production Board

WRAC Women's Royal Army Corps

WRAF Women's Royal Air Force

WRENS, W.R.N.S. Women's Royal Naval Service (Brit.)

wrnt. warrant

WSW west-southwest

wt. weight

W. Va. West Virginia

WVS Women's Voluntary Service (Brit.)

WW I, WW II World War I; World War II

Wyo., Wy. Wyoming

X

X Christ; Christian; ten (Roman numeral); xenon

x an abscissa; an unknown quantity

X.C., x.c., x-cp ex coupon

X.D., x.d., x-div. ex dividend

Xe xenon (Chem.)

X.i., x-i., x-int. ex-interest

Xmas Christmas

Xn. Christian

Xnty., Xty. Christianity

XP Latinized monogram for the Greek word for Christ.

X-rts. ex-rights

Xtian. Christian

Y

Y yttrium (Chem.)

Y, Y. YMCA, YMHA, YWCA, (with "the")

y an unknown quantity (Math.)

y. yard; yards; year; years

Yale L.J. Yale Law Journal

Y.B. yearbook

Yb ytterbium (Chem.)

Y.C.L. Young Communist League

yd. yard

yds. yards

ydg. yarding

Yem. Yemen

yeo. yeomanry

yesty. yesterday

Y1c Yeoman first class

YHA Youth Hostels Association

Yidd. Yiddish

yieldg. yielding

Yks. Yorkshire

Y.M.C.A. Young Men's Christian Association

Y.M.Cath.A. Young Men's Catholic Association

Y.M.H.A. Young Men's Hebrew Association

YMS Motor Minesweepers (USN)

YN Yeoman (USN)

y.o. year old

Yorks Yorkshire (England)

y.p. yield point; yield limit

Y.P.S.C.E. Young People's Society of Christian Endeavor

Y.P.S.L. Young People's Socialist League. An early acronymic, pronounced **yipsil**. Its arch-rival, the Y.C.L., however, pronounced each letter with the full value.

yr. year; your; younger

y.s. yard super; yield strength

y.t. yoke top

Yt yttrium (Chem.)

Y.T. Yukon Territory (Canada)

Y3c Yeoman third class (USN)

Y.U. Yale University; Yeshiva University

Yuc. Yucatan (Mexico)

Yugo. Yugoslavia

Yuk. Yukon

Y.W. Young Women's Christian Association (with "the")

Y.W.C.A. Young Women's Christian Association

Y.W.H.A. Young Women's Hebrew Association

Z

Z atomic number (Chem.); zenith distance (Astron.); zone (used in combination only, US Army)

z an unknown quantity (Math.)

z. zero; zone

Zac. Zacatecas (Mexico)

Zach. Zacharias (Biblical); Zachary

Zan. Zanzibar

Zeb. Zebedee

Zech. Zecharaiah (Biblical)

Zeph. Zephaniah (Biblical)

Z.G. Zoological Gardens

ZI Zone of Interior (US Army)

zl. zloty, the monetary unit of Poland

Zn zinc (Chem.)

Z.O.A. Zionist Organization of America

zoochem. zoochemistry

zoogeog. zoogeography

zool. zoological; zoology

zooph. zoophytology

Zor. Zoroastrian; Zoroastrianism

Zr zirconium (Chem.)

Bibliography

Allen, E. F. *Allen's Dictionary of Abbreviations and Symbols.* New York: Coward-McCann. 1946.

Collins, F. H. *Authors' and Printers' Dictionary.* 10th edition. London: Oxford University Press. 1956.

De Sola, Ralph. *Abbreviations Dictionary.* New York: Duell, Sloan and Pearce. 1958.

United States Government Printing Office Style Manual. (GPO). Revised edition. Washington. 1959. Pp. 155-162 contain an excellent list of standard abbreviations. On p. 162 is the best brief statement on "uniform treatment in the formation of coined words and symbols."

Partridge, Eric. *Dictionary of Abbreviations.* London: Allen & Unwin. 1949.

Schwartz, Robert J. *The Complete Dictionary of Abbreviations.* New York: Crowell. 1955.

Shankle, G. E. *Current Abbreviations.* New York: H. W. Wilson. 1945.

Stephenson, H. J. *Abbrevs: A Dictionary of Abbreviations.* New York: Macmillan. 1943.

World List of Abbreviations (of scientific, technological and commercial organizations). London: Leonard Hill. 1960.

N.B. Most modern general dictionaries, encyclopedias, publications of learned, scientific and professional societies, etc. contain a list of abbreviations used in each work.